LET'S ROLL THIS TRAIN

To John
Brown
I am glad to
have you as
a friend

Leslon

LET'S ROLL THIS TRAIN

My Life in New Mexico Education, Business, and Politics

LENTON MALRY

UNIVERSITY OF NEW MEXICO PRESS | ALBUQUERQUE

Library of Congress Cataloging-in-Publication Data
Names: Malry, Lenton, 1931– author.
Title: Let's roll this train : my life in New Mexico education, business, and politics / Lenton Malry.
Other titles: My life in New Mexico education, business, and politics
Description: Albuquerque : University of New Mexico Press, [2016] | Includes index.
Identifiers: LCCN 2015045707 (print) | LCCN 2015046958 (ebook) |
ISBN 9780826357434 (pbk. : alk. paper) | ISBN 9780826357441 (Electronic)
Subjects: LCSH: Malry, Lenton, 1931– | Politicians—New Mexico—Biography. | Educators—
New Mexico—Biography. | African Americans—New Mexico—Biography. |
Legislators—New Mexico—Biography. | New Mexico. Legislature. House of
Representatives—Biography. | New Mexico—Politics and government—1951– |
New Mexico—Race relations—Anecdotes. | Bernalillo County (N.M.)—Biography.
Classification: LCC F801.4.M39 A3 2016 (print) | LCC F801.4.M39 (ebook) |
DDC 328.73/092—dc23
LC record available at http://lccn.loc.gov/2015045707

Cover photograph courtesy of Lenton Malry
Designed by Felicia Cedillos
Composed in Minion Pro 10.5/14.5

All images are courtesy of the Malry family collection except where otherwise indicated.

The Center for Regional Studies at the University of New Mexico generously
provided funding to support publication of this book.

Contents

Foreword

For ten years Representative Lenton Malry sat with his sidekicks in the New Mexico legislature—icons like Raymond Sanchez, Joe Lang, Aubrey Dunn, and a host of other *hombres* (men). He became a member of the group of intellectuals who headed a thundering herd of education advocates that included Governors Jerry Apodaca and Bruce King. Malry was a leader in supporting education on all levels.

As the president of the University of New Mexico from 1975 to 1982, I can attest to the fact that the university was one of the beneficiaries of his tireless and effective leadership.

I look back on my forty years of association with Malry with pride and gratitude for his efforts. In my time at the university, Malry made good things happen. Between 1978 and 1981 the University of New Mexico received $3.8 million in supplementary appropriations for hospital equipment and $300,000 in supplementary funding for library acquisitions. In 1980 the legislature approved a special supplementary appropriation of $5 million per year to upgrade the science and engineering laboratories at all the state universities. In 1982 the University of New Mexico ranked third nationally in the increase of appropriations for higher education (131 percent), faculty salaries had increased 65 percent in six years, and the university began more than $57 million worth of new construction. Approximately 170 new faculty slots were added on the main campus. These things didn't just happen. Good people like Lenton Malry made them happen through leadership, oratory, and, on appropriate occasions, arm-twisting.

If you ramble around New Mexico, you will find that Representative Lenton Malry is a noted name. Black, not Hispanic, he is what Latinos and Native Americans in the state call a *tybo*, which means a "black white man." Whatever! The state's combined minority population—African Americans, Hispanics, and Native Americans—accounts for 55 percent of the population. Together these groups form a powerful bloc in any legislative session. And often, by voting as a bloc, they could and did make good things happen, such as supporting education on all levels. During his time in state government, Malry was one of the prominent leaders in this voting bloc.

Despite his sometimes modest self-image, Malry is not the ace of spades or even the king of hearts. He is too muscular to be the queen of diamonds. His main forte is his role as the jack of clubs: he wallops with a heavy hand.

In his early life he had great mentors, including perhaps one of the nation's premier football coaches, Grambling College's Eddie Robinson (whose dictum was that if you didn't go to church on Sunday, you wouldn't get in the game the next Saturday).

Malry's time in the US Air Force also changed his life. His superior officers (if there were any) didn't care what color he was—they demanded efficiency, diligence, and intelligence. And while his compadres frittered away their off-duty hours in bars and taverns, Malry took advantage of his time with the British Army Air Corps to study in some of the best English universities. The elegance of England rubbed off on the maverick Malry.

Malry's leadership has not been confined to New Mexico. He is a hero of the Mountain West and has been a leader in higher education for the entire West. As the president of the Western Interstate Commission for Higher Education (WICHE), he came to know the governors and legislators in every western state, and he traveled to the great public universities and colleges in each one to study them. Not every state in the West has a medical school or a college of dentistry or veterinary medicine. Through WICHE, Malry paved the way for the graduates of universities in the "have-not" states to get their doctoral degrees through admission to professional graduate schools in other states in the West.

Malry even helped convince the sometimes reluctant legislative bodies to pay the tab for the out-of-state students who were admitted to these programs. So when a medical doctor is setting a broken bone, a dentist is filling or pulling a tooth, or a veterinarian is caring for a sick horse, one should think of and give thanks for the leadership of Malry.

Throughout his life Lenton Malry has had a special passion for education. As a student, a teacher, an administrator, and a legislator, he has touched all the bases and taken advantage of the opportunities that came his way.

Today he is a shining example of what an individual at his or her best might be. The narrative of his journey to become one of New Mexico's living legends should be an inspiration to those who would aspire to learn and serve and lead.

William E. Davis
FORMER PRESIDENT
University of New Mexico

Preface

It is not unique that I have a story to tell. Everyone in this world does. Some simply have more to say than others. However, it is not common for a person to write his or her story as an autobiography.

The reason I have written my story is to answer questions often asked by my family and friends. I considered that now was the most opportune time to write the details, while my memory is still relatively clear.

The story begins with a poor black child living on a small farm in rural northwest Louisiana, and then it traces the paths that led to my attending high school in Shreveport, attending Grambling College at age sixteen, graduating, joining the air force, and then being stationed in London, England. The story then weaves its way back to the United States, where I began teaching at Texas College and met the woman who would become my wife, Joy Dell Green. Next I chronicle our experience teaching and living on the Navajo reservation before moving to Albuquerque, New Mexico, where I continued my professional teaching life and began my political life. Finally I discuss my retirement and some thoughts about my journey.

Overall it was a pleasure to write this story. There were challenges during the three years it took me to write it, consisting mainly of writer's fatigue and the forgetting of certain events. But these challenges were overcome by the drive and inspiration that I had to tell my story for the benefit of my family.

I have tried to tell a simple, straightforward story, with little or no attempt at embellishment. I wrestled with the notion of embellishment because I did not want to appear as a braggadocio, but at the same time I wanted to provide a bit of inspiration for those who may question whether they themselves can accomplish many of the things that I was blessed to accomplish through my Lord Jesus Christ.

Acknowledgments

I would like to express my gratitude to the many people who saw me through this book; to all those who provided support, talked things over, read, wrote, offered comments, and assisted in the editing, proofreading, and design.

Above all I want to thank my wife, Joy, and my son, Lenton Jr., who supported and encouraged me in spite of all the time it took me away from them.

I would like to thank Franchesca Stevenson for helping me to edit the early portion of the book; my son, Lenton Jr., for editing; and John W. Byram, the director of the University of New Mexico Press, for his critical role in selecting, editing, encouraging, and assisting in the publishing of the book.

I am grateful to the New Mexico Legislative Council Service, specifically Tracy Kimball, the librarian who assisted me with research data.

Last and not least, I beg the forgiveness of all those who have been with me over the course of these years and whose names I have failed to mention.

CHAPTER 1

The Early Years

⌒办⌒

"Let's roll this train" was a catchphrase I used in the 1980s when I was the chairman of the Bernalillo County Commission. I'd use it whenever I wanted my fellow commissioners to stop talking and arrive at a decision. More often than not it worked, by causing us to refocus and move the agenda forward more quickly.

I never minded hard work. I've literally and figuratively plowed more fields in my life than I care to remember. I was the first in my family to graduate from college, and I was the first black person to receive a PhD in education administration from the University of New Mexico. My wife and I were the first black family to integrate Albuquerque's Ridgecrest neighborhood in the Southeast Heights and the first black members of the First Baptist Church on the edge of downtown Albuquerque. I served as the first black male teacher and the first black school principal in the Albuquerque Public School District. In addition, I was the first black state legislator in New Mexico's history as well as the first black Bernalillo county commissioner. All of these were accomplishments that I never dreamed could or would happen to me when I was a child working on my parents' farm near Shreveport, Louisiana.

My father, James Malry, grew up on a cotton and corn plantation in East Texas. He left the farm in 1919, when he was eighteen years old, and moved to Keithville, Louisiana, just south of Shreveport. Attending church one Sunday, Dad met my mother, Mary Ansley, and they quickly became inseparable.

They married and then purchased a forty-acre farm with money that my dad's white father, the plantation owner, had given him. My parents had three boys: John, the eldest; Clinton; and me, the youngest, born in 1931. The environment at home was one of love, hard work, and a Christian spirit.

Growing up in the 1930s, my brothers and I attended a two-room segregated elementary school. One teacher taught first through third grades, and the other taught grades four through six. Most of our time outside the classroom was spent working on the farm, plowing the field, and taking care of the animals. This was a typical occurrence until I attended high school.

Our farm was roughly 80 percent contained, which means that we produced just about everything we needed to survive. We grew our own crops for consumption, such as corn, potatoes, greens, and tomatoes, and we sold corn and cotton. We also raised cattle, hogs, and chickens to eat and sell.

Every day my brothers and I each had a specific job assignment. John would feed the horses and donkeys, Clinton would feed the hogs, and because I was the youngest I had the easiest job, which was feeding the chickens. All I had to do was simply throw the grain out to them. I didn't have to lift the heavy bales of hay for the horses and donkeys, or step in the mud with the hogs. Dad was the supervisor, continually monitoring us. This was how hard work was instilled in me. My mom was busy doing chores in the house, including preparing the evening meal. She was a great cook.

About once a month my dad would borrow a truck, and our family would travel north to Shreveport, which was about twenty miles from the farm, to buy food that we didn't produce. This included items such as sugar, lard, flour, cornmeal, and syrup. As a treat my parents would give my brothers and me money to go to the movies while they shopped for groceries and ran errands. I really enjoyed the movies and looked forward to seeing a new one each time we went into town. One movie I remember seeing and being thoroughly entertained by was *Santa Fe Trail*, starring Ronald Reagan.

After the movie we would look for a restaurant that served black people, since this was in the midst of the Jim Crow era. More often than not it was a Chinese restaurant located on Central Avenue. For about thirty-five cents I would get a sausage and rice plate, and for an additional fifteen cents I would treat myself to a pint of vanilla ice cream. I can certainly trace the origins of my sweet tooth, for ice cream in particular, to when I was very young. After the fun afternoon, we would travel back to the farm and continue the chores, such as feeding the animals, before going to bed.

On some Saturday afternoons when we didn't go to Shreveport, my brothers and I would walk four miles to the local John Gin Store, named for the road on which it was located. Here we would buy baloney and treat ourselves to a soda pop—for me, always strawberry flavored, my favorite.

Television was in its infancy in the 1930s, so radio was the primary source of entertainment. Many families in our area did not own a radio. We were fortunate, however, that my father owned a large Firestone radio. In the evenings after dinner we enjoyed gathering around it and listening to music, news, and other events. I fondly remember listening to the Joe Louis boxing matches as well. Listening to the radio was a social event for my family. My parents really enjoyed having friends over to visit; many area farmers would come over to our home to enjoy eating, socializing, and listening to music or the fights. Many times there would be more than twenty people gathered in our backyard.

As for many people in our area, transportation was a challenge for us. My family didn't own a vehicle. We needed to borrow one, or when my father needed some small item like tobacco he would send me to the store on my bicycle. I remember that while I was in the fourth grade my parents provided accommodations for two teachers from the local elementary school for one year. The teachers lived at our house during the week because they didn't have a car, so they couldn't go home to Shreveport until Friday afternoon, for the weekend.

My maternal grandmother, Leah Ansley, also lived on a farm about a mile away, but her farm was smaller than ours. In an effort to support her, since her husband had died, I would often pick some tomatoes or cucumbers from our fields and take them to her. She appreciated the support, and it provided me the opportunity to visit with her, which I really enjoyed. In addition to hearing her tell stories of her and my mother growing up, I fondly recall that while she was eating fruit she would call out to me, "Boy, come here and sit in front of me." As I anxiously sat on the floor, she would peel an apple and give me the skin. Sometimes she cut deeper into the apple to provide me with more of the fruit. I was very excited and appreciative. What a foreign concept this must be to today's generation of children needing to be entertained.

I would also play with Janie Mae Jack, my first cousin, who lived next door to Grandmother Ansley. Janie Mae was two years older than me. We were very close, and she was protective of me, even from bullies at school. Once when some boys were picking a fight with me, Janie Mae defended me by stepping in and actually beating one of them up! She didn't have to punch all of them, just the biggest one.

Another childhood friend of mine was a schoolmate named Booker T. Bennett who lived about two miles from my home. The Bennetts were an upper-middle-class family who owned a very large farm and several cars. Robert Bennett, the father, really believed in the value of education. He was constantly checking on his children's progress in school. He had five children, and they all attended college.

It was my parents' emphasis on education, reinforced by Mr. Bennett, that provided me with the foundation, interest, and desire to continually strive to learn and attend college. There were, however, some lighter moments in the Bennett household.

One day when I was visiting Booker T. his family invited me to stay for lunch. Unbeknownst to me, his sister, Versia Mae, had cut some okra and asked her mother to fry it for her for lunch. Betty Bennett asked me if I wanted some, and I said, "Yes, thank you." A not-too-happy Versia Mae pointedly stated, "Mom, I cut that okra for me!" But her mother gave me half anyway. Booker T. laughed, causing Versia Mae to become more upset, and a sibling argument ensued, all because of me. Several years later, while we were both attending the same college, Versia Mae would playfully remind me of that story.

The Bennetts played an important part in my educational pursuit by providing transportation. While I was in junior high school they would give me rides home from school. Otherwise I would have had to walk about six miles. I could always hitch a ride to class in the morning, but I needed a way to get home. Although I was grateful, those rides back weren't always that much fun. When the car was full, I would have to stand outside on the running board. It would have been okay to have the wind blowing in my face for a mile, but six miles was a bit much. To pay Mr. Bennett back, my dad would give him beef and other food items from our farm, because he didn't have any money. During this time the black children had to provide their own transportation to Spring Hill Junior High School, whereas the white children, who went to a different school (in this case Greenwood High School) had bus transportation provided for them.

I'm a Christian. Aside from emphasizing education, my parents instilled in me the importance of believing in God. Attending church was therefore a big part of my life. We were members of Cross Road Baptist Church, and my mother sang in the choir. She would insist that my brother Clinton and I attend church every Sunday, so we would leave home early in the morning to attend Sunday school and the larger church service. It provided me, at a young age, with the opportunity to socialize with my friends. At times Clinton would assume big-brother responsibilities by disciplining me in Sunday school when I was more interested in socializing than in paying attention to the lesson.

After the services there was plenty of time to socialize, and occasionally we would attend a church picnic. There were large amounts of food, including beef, chicken, and tasty desserts like my favorite, ice cream. The adults would have a great time socializing while the children ran around playing games like baseball.

Every Monday morning we went back to school, and after school we went back to the fields. School was certainly different in many ways back then, one of which was in the area of discipline. Teachers were allowed to be the authority figures in the absence of the parents. I'll never forget the time in first grade when my teacher, Mildred Curliff, disciplined me by whipping me after school. I had continually been talking and socializing, but because I was the youngest, the "baby" of the family, I didn't think she had any right to whip me; only my parents had that right. So when I got home that day, I proceeded to tell Dad what had happened. Dad was just coming in from the field with a plow and rope, and he was clearly not in the greatest of moods. I told him that Mrs. Curliff had punished me after class, so he asked, "What did you do?" I was silent. Dad then said, "Come here," and he proceeded to whip me again. I mean, he whipped the heck out of me. After that I behaved better in the classroom, and the few times I was disciplined after that, I never informed my dad. Today Mrs. Curliff and my cousin Janie Mae attend the same church in Shreveport. Mrs. Curliff, who recently celebrated her 102nd birthday, asked for a photograph of me, which I gladly sent her.

I skipped second grade because Mrs. Curliff believed that I was advanced enough at that time to enter third grade. After finishing the sixth grade, several students did not attend junior high school solely because of the lack of transportation. Even fewer students attended high school, for the same reason. Because the Bennett family provided me with transportation, I was able to complete the seventh, eighth, and ninth grades at Spring Hill Junior High School.

The Bennett family couldn't continue to provide me with transportation during my high school years, however, and this forced me to move in with my aunt, Mattie Ansley. My parents viewed education as a priority for me, and we were fortunate to have my mom's sister living in Shreveport close to the high school. At that time high school consisted only of the tenth and eleventh grades (there was no twelfth grade until the state law changed in 1949).

During my first year with Aunt Mattie, Dad would pick me up every Friday afternoon and take me back to the farm. I would work on Friday until dark, then all day Saturday. As usual, on Sunday we went to church. Then on Monday morning, Dad would take me back to Aunt Mattie's house. He believed that it was more important for me to attend high school than to help him on the farm. In addition to allowing me to avoid working full-time on the farm, this also continued to instill in me the seriousness and the value of education, and I didn't want to let my parents down.

The next year, when I was a senior (in eleventh grade), I got a job as a busboy at the Washington Hotel in Shreveport, where I worked during the week from 4:00 to 11:30 p.m. I wanted to save money for college. I remember that my supervisor was really nice and understanding. She understood that I was going to school, so when work was slow she would allow me to study.

I was sixteen when I graduated from high school, and I worked a double shift at the hotel that summer, from 7:00 a.m. to 11:00 p.m. I would catch up on sleep on the weekends. Within about three months I had saved enough money for one semester of college, approximately $150.

Living in Shreveport was certainly a culture shock for me on a number of levels. It was my first experience of being integrated with whites on a daily basis, and at Central High School I experienced a different group of black students. They were called Creoles, generally a lighter-skinned people of mixed French and black heritage, descendants of the original French settlers of Louisiana and free blacks. The Creole students attended private Catholic schools from grades one through nine and were taught by white nuns. In the tenth grade they had to attend the black high school, and the transition was very hard for some of them.

For example, a concerned parent, Johnny Williams, who owned a funeral home, asked the city council to create three seating arrangements on the city buses. The front section would be for whites, the middle section for Creoles and light-skinned blacks, and the back section for dark-skinned blacks. The city council turned him down. It was strange to me that most of those students would associate only with other light-skinned blacks. Some of them were friendly to me but not to my brother Clinton, who was darker-skinned. I didn't appreciate that.

Many black people who grew up with me believed that light-skinned blacks were superior to dark-skinned blacks. I saw this at Central High School, and I also saw it when I went to college. I had grown accustomed to being treated differently by whites, but this behavior by blacks was really puzzling.

CHAPTER 2

College

⌒*⌒*

When I graduated from Central High School in Shreveport in the spring of 1948, there were four black colleges in Louisiana: Southern University in Baton Rouge, 280 miles from Shreveport; Dillard University, a private school in New Orleans, more than 200 miles from Shreveport; Xavier University, a Roman Catholic school, also in New Orleans; and Grambling College in the town of Grambling, about 60 miles from Shreveport.

I decided to enroll at Grambling College because of its proximity to home and the fact that many of my friends were planning to go there. Some of my more affluent friends chose to attend Texas College in Tyler, Texas; Fisk University in Nashville, Tennessee; or other black private schools. I was fortunate to be able to attend the college of my choice.

Founded in 1901 and accredited in 1949, the college was named after a white sawmill owner, Judson H. Grambling, who donated a parcel of land for the school. Grambling was founded as a teachers' college and offered courses in science, liberal arts, and business. I decided to focus on rural-teaching education.

In the fall of 1948 I was a sixteen-year-old freshman. All the other students at Grambling College were older. To say that I was apprehensive, anxious, and in some respects scared would be an understatement. It wasn't the first time I had been away from home, but it was certainly the first time I was away from my family. I prayed a lot, and the Lord answered my prayers, again in the form of the Bennett family. My former grade school friend Booker T., who was in his second year at Grambling, became my roommate in the dormitory. His older brother, Robert Lee Bennett, a senior, checked on us regularly to make sure we were okay. Their sister, Versia Mae (the one who had been upset with me for eating her okra), was on campus too, and she offered guidance and support when it was needed. Booker T. and I would eat at the campus cafeteria, study at the library, and attend church services together every Sunday. I greatly appreciate the support the Bennett family gave me, and to this day I maintain contact with Booker T., who is retired from teaching and resides in Lake Charles, Louisiana.

During the first semester my classes consisted of American history, English fundamentals, general math, physical education, and biological science. This was a total of sixteen credit hours. Although having a job in high school had taught me how to budget my time, it still took me awhile to adjust to a college environment. As a result my classwork in my first year was only average. I improved steadily as a student thereafter.

There were many people at Grambling College who supported and inspired me, but two particularly come to mind. One was a teacher in the Education Department. She was a very young instructor named Helen Richardson who had graduated from Grambling College a couple of years before I arrived. She received her master's degree from Columbia University in New York City and later earned a PhD from Columbia as well. She always encouraged me to believe in myself and aim high.

Another person who constantly encouraged me to set and achieve high goals was the assistant registrar, Ruby Weekly. When I first met her I was a student employee, responsible for cleaning the offices of three administrators: the registrar, the dean of the College of Education, and the business manager. Mrs. Weekly provided positive reinforcement by saying, "You're smart, and you're going places." She was a wonderful woman whom I keep in touch with to this day. I visited her a few years ago when I went back to Grambling for my induction into the school's Hall of Fame.

In my first year at Grambling College, Major Colton, the maintenance director, gave me a job. I never knew whether *Major* was really his first name or just what everybody called him because he used to be in the military. He was another person who thought highly of me and supported me, by arranging for me to get a work scholarship for the remainder of my college years. When I first enrolled at Grambling I had enough money to attend for only one year. After that I was able to pay for my room, meals, and tuition by working. I owe a great amount of gratitude to Major, for he kept me in school.

When I first received a work scholarship, I, along with four other young men, would meet and clean classrooms from 3:00 to 5:00 p.m. five days a week. At the end of the first year I earned a promotion. Major informed me that the following fall I would be assigned to three offices downstairs. This was significant because I did not have to begin at 3:00 p.m. I could clean the offices anytime before 8:00 a.m. the next day, which allowed me to study during the day after my classes ended. My job performance was good and was often praised by the secretaries. I was grateful to have the job, since it allowed me to stay in school.

There was not much social life in Grambling, and the next closest town was Ruston, three miles away. About once a month there was a dance on campus, which I looked forward to. I would dress in my best suit—I only had two, and this one was blue; I wore it with a white shirt and a red tie to impress my date and others. Many schoolmates commented that I looked very patriotic!

Grambling was located in Lincoln Parish; a parish is an administrative subdivision in Louisiana that corresponds to a county in other states. Lincoln Parish was also a dry parish—one could not purchase any alcoholic beverages there. Occasionally some guys would travel outside the parish and purchase a gallon of wine and sell it for twenty cents a glass. It really didn't interest me, but it did allow me some relief from studying and an opportunity to socialize with the guys. I had three roommates: Theodore Foster, Leon Holt, and my best friend from home, Booker T. Bennett. Holt and Foster were from Bunkie, Louisiana. After Leon graduated he taught school in his hometown and later became principal of Bunkie High School. I'm not really sure what happened to Theodore. I heard that he moved up north—maybe to Michigan—to work in the automobile industry. Booker T. began teaching in Lake Charles, Louisiana, and was then drafted into the Korean War. He later returned to teach in Lake Charles.

I'd be remiss if I didn't mention Lee Flentroy, my physical-education teacher. I really enjoyed his classes and received high praise and good grades from him. He suggested that I try out for the football team—Hall of Fame coach Eddie Robinson's football team.

Grambling's football teams were legendary. During Coach Robinson's fifty-seven-year career, the school gained a national reputation because of the large number of players who went on to join the professional ranks, including Willie Brown, Buck Buchanan, Willie Davis, Charlie Joiner, and Doug Williams, a quarterback who led the Washington Redskins to a Super Bowl championship. Coach Robinson achieved the National Collegiate Athletic Association (NCAA) record for most career wins as the head coach at an NCAA Division I school. When he retired in 1997 his record was 408 wins, 165 losses, and 15 ties.

I went out for spring practice for a few weeks but wasn't invited back in the fall. I was a running back, and the team already had plenty of them. I weighed about 170 pounds, and the other running backs typically weighed well over 200 pounds.

For the few weeks that I was in spring training, I lived in a special football dormitory. I remember fondly that Coach Robinson would come through the dormitory at 6:00 a.m. ringing a big cowbell and shouting, "It's time to get up and go to class." He would also make us attend church every Sunday.

Unlike at home, in Grambling there were many types of churches to attend: Baptist, Methodist, Catholic, and Presbyterian. I usually went to the Baptist church, but some of the other guys went to the Catholic church because the worship service was shorter, only about an hour. The Baptist service was typically two hours. At the end of my freshman year I went back to Shreveport to live with Aunt Mattie and to work at the Washington Hotel.

I didn't want to work on the farm anymore. It was hard work, and Dad was working only about half of the fields by then. He had taken a job at the local sawmill.

It was also my last summer working at the hotel. Each summer Major Colton would keep a few students to work at the college over the summer. After my first year I was fortunate to be selected as part of the summer workforce. The highlight of that summer was that I learned how to drive.

The college used a Chevrolet truck to haul and deliver supplies like lumber and bags of concrete for construction jobs. I was always the first one to get in the driver's seat—I was eager to drive. The distances were not very far, just down some country roads. One morning, though, I backed the truck into a car. We were getting ready to do a job, and I didn't look around to see what was behind me. I was just learning to drive. To make matters worse, the owner of the car was standing there talking to Major at the time! Obviously embarrassed, I apologized and offered to pay for the damage. At the end of the month this minor accident cost me ten dollars, taken out of my paycheck.

I have a lot of good memories of working at school. One night we laid some concrete in a building, and Major ordered a bunch of hamburgers for us to eat when we were finished. After we ate, he dismissed everyone on the crew except for me and Ben, one of the other workers. He gave us some extra hamburgers and discussed school and our future plans. I knew then that he understood I was younger than the others and that he was trying to be a good example.

In my junior and senior years I was very well adjusted to campus life. My boss trusted me with keys to the front door of the administration building. In the back was the football field. On Friday nights the black high schools played their games there. I would clean the offices and take some of my friends to help, then I would let them out the back door to see the football games for free.

I was also a member of the Grambling Theatre Guild. We traveled to many high schools to put on plays, and we also performed at the college. Most of our performances were within one hundred miles, although once we went to New Iberia, more than two hundred miles away. My main job was to set up for the shows, but I was also in a few plays. I guess I wasn't cut out to be a professional actor, though. One time, in a play at Grambling, I forgot my lines and started making things up. If that wasn't bad enough, out of frustration I used some off-color language. Needless to say, after that I relegated myself to my main job of stagehand.

During my junior year my brother Clinton enrolled at Grambling. He attended college on the GI Bill after being in the army, and I was glad to have him join me on campus. Clinton had gone to Southern University for a few years and then transferred to Grambling to be closer to home. Clinton had a car, which was significant to me, given my history of transportation challenges. I was dating a bit, and for fun on some weekends we would go to Monroe, about forty miles away, to have dinner and see a movie. This is also where I first saw blues guitarist B. B. King perform. We had a great time. Clinton stayed at Grambling State for only one year, though, then he married Myrtis Street and moved back to Shreveport, where he got a job and started a beautiful family. Clinton and Myrtis have three children: Sondera, Constance, and Clinton Jr.

In my senior year my attentiveness to studying was about to pay off: I was finally getting close to graduating. My courses included teaching science, arithmetic, social studies, and language in elementary school, and problems in education. In the summer of 1952 I did my student teaching on campus, at Grambling's demonstration school. I really enjoyed teaching the fourth-grade students, which I did for nine weeks.

I graduated from Grambling College in August 1952, and the Korean War was in full force then. I had been deferred from the military until graduation. When I returned home from college, I received a letter from the draft board requiring me to come in for a visit. I really did not want to go into the army, because some of my friends had been drafted, and after they completed basic training they were sent directly to Korea. When I had my meeting with the recruiter, I was told to return the following week and take a group of tests, which I did. The recruiter gave me a choice: I could enlist in the army for two years or in the air force for four years. I had one week to make my decision. Most black men went into the army. The air force at that time was only about 10 to 15 percent black. I conferred with my family and friends and prayed on it deeply. On October 15, 1952, I enlisted in the US Air Force. It was one of the best decisions I ever made.

The benefits, in my view, were that I could continue my education and travel overseas, both great opportunities. I also thought that the blue uniform was impressive. My older brothers served in the army and the navy, and I wanted something different. I was excited to go to training.

I think I got my drive and determination from both my parents, but especially from my mom. In church she not only sang in the choir, she also headed the crew that put on the Christmas plays. She was very strong willed and was adept at directing people. That may be where I got my early interest in the theater. Yet education was important to her. I distinctly remember one time: I was getting ready to go to high school, but Dad thought I was going to work in the fields. Mom sternly said, "No, he's going to school." She was a very wise woman. She didn't go beyond grade school, but she always told my brothers and me that the key to success is to get an education. She said that it would open doors for black people, "and I want you to be part of it." That was Mary Malry.

CHAPTER 3

The US Air Force, 1952–1956

$\mathcal{M}$

I didn't know much about San Antonio, Texas. I had read that the city was very historic. I also knew it was called the Alamo City in honor of the famous Battle of the Alamo, the pivotal event of the Texas Revolution in 1836.

On the evening of October 14, 1952, I packed a few things in preparation for leaving the next morning to serve my country for four years. My mother came in my room to pray with me. She knelt on the floor and prayed, and the phrase I remember most was "God, protect my son while he is in the military." As she fought back tears she stood up and hugged and kissed me. It really touched me. Both of my older brothers had served in the military, John in the navy and Clinton in the army. Although they had given me advice, I still had a hard time sleeping that night because I didn't know what to expect. I knew that basic training would be a life-changing experience for me, my first full racial-integration experience. The only advice really given to me was to "just be careful." I thought, careful of what? So I decided to be careful of almost everything.

The next morning, after saying good-bye to Mom and Dad, I boarded a train in Shreveport for San Antonio. When I arrived that evening I was taken to Lackland Air Force Base for nine weeks of basic training. Although the military was still segregated during World War II, when my brothers had served, in 1948 President Harry Truman signed an executive order desegregating the armed forces. The order had been in effect for four years, but since the rest of society was still segregated, this was my first experience with integration. My fellow enlistees and I all lived in open barracks and did everything together. Each barrack consisted of one large room with about fifty people in a squadron. In my barrack, approximately ten of us were black. It was awkward, but I tried to maintain my focus on the job at hand, which was to learn the importance of discipline, teamwork, the chain of command, and the foundational knowledge one would need to succeed as an airman. I kept all of this in mind in the context of serving my country.

One thing I didn't have to adjust to was waking up early. Every morning except Sunday the technical instructor would wake us up at the break of dawn and give us thirty minutes to shower and dress. This brought back memories of when I was on the farm and Dad would get me up early to plow the fields. Dad never gave me thirty minutes to get dressed, though; it was more like ten minutes.

Basic training included lots of marching, both early in the morning and in the evening. Talk about working up an appetite! Another component of basic training was pistol and rifle training. I was not a great marksman by any stretch of the imagination. But I was a relatively fast learner because back on the farm in Louisiana Dad and I would often go rabbit hunting on weekends. Once as I was practicing, I was nervous about being watched and I wasn't able to hold the rifle straight; it kept shifting back and forth. The trainer came over to me and said, "You gotta hold that thing straight, nigger." I was shocked, and this certainly added to my distractions! I notified my supervisor, and it never happened again.

We really didn't have many major racial problems in the squadron, just slight differences. This was illustrated, for example, in our preferences in music. When we were allowed to listen to the radio, the white guys wanted to listen to bluegrass or country-and-western music. We blacks wanted to listen to jazz. So everyone tried to blast the others out. Something had to give, and eventually the tactical instructor, our commander, called all of us together. "Listen," he said. "You're going to have to get along, so turn it down. Put your ears closer to the radios."

There were other minor incidents as well, since all of us were adjusting to integration. But ultimately the threat of punishment by the tactical instructor was enough to curb bad behavior. I realized that the military was the perfect place to institute integration, because we all had to follow orders.

Generally, after a full day of training, we had a little time off in the evening. It was common for me to sit outside the mess hall and strike up a conversation with the new airmen, beginning with asking them where they were from. I met two or three who were from Shreveport, but I didn't pursue friendships with them because they were white. I mostly socialized with the black servicemen while slowly adjusting to integration.

After five weeks in basic training, we were given passes to go into the city. I was eager to visit and, along with two of my friends, I ventured into San Antonio. Several soldiers were interested in meeting girls, but remembering what my brothers and others had advised me about being careful, I didn't want to go to the seedier parts of the city, out of safety concerns. Besides, I was excited to see the historical part of San Antonio. We visited the San Antonio Museum and, of course, the Alamo.

After nine weeks it was time to move to another base: Barksdale Air Force Base in Shreveport. I had mixed emotions. I was glad to be going home, but I also really wanted to live in a new place. I was hoping to get an assignment somewhere like California, to see some of the other parts of the country and, eventually, the world. As it turned out, there were ten of us going from Lackland to Barksdale.

We packed and went to the bus station in San Antonio. As expected, we black soldiers went to the "colored section" of the bus station to check in while the six white airmen checked in at the whites-only section. After the white airmen received their tickets, they waited for us. We all boarded at the same time, and the four of us black airmen headed toward the back of the bus. After I was seated I looked around and saw that the six white airmen were in the back of the bus with us. They were trying to send a message to everyone that we shouldn't segregate. The bus driver didn't say anything. We were all in uniform. The civilians kept looking back, but no one said anything to the white airmen to make them move. It made me feel like integration was really beginning to take effect. I didn't know if it would last, but it made me feel good to know that these guys wanted to be with us, and I told them I appreciated it.

After I checked in at Barksdale, I anxiously went to see my mom and dad. They had sold the farm and moved into a very nice home in a new subdivision. A developer from New York had come to Shreveport and built about twenty new homes in a black subdivision. This was in 1952, and it was the first time that black people in Shreveport could own a new home unless they had built it themselves; until then, they couldn't just buy one. It was very nice and it was a far cry from what I had grown up in.

Our farmhouse had had no plumbing and no electricity, so this was a complete transformation. Mom and Dad's one-story house cost about $10,000. They sold the farmhouse and forty acres for $3,000 to $4,000 and used that money as a down payment on the new house. About twenty years ago, I went back to see the old farm. It was a good experience to revisit the area where I grew up. I had so many happy times there.

On my first visit home while in the air force, Dad hugged me as always and Mom cried tears of joy. Many relatives came to see me, and we had a fun celebration. Mom made barbecued ribs, buffalo fish, and peach cobbler. It was the first time they had seen me in uniform, standing proud and representing our country. It felt good being home with my family.

Dad was then having difficulty finding a full-time job, but he kept working part-time at the sawmills. Mom, a good cook, had a full-time cooking job at Centenary College in Shreveport. To help them pay their bills, I would give them about forty dollars a month.

My brothers were moving on as well. John would not live in the South again after he got out of the navy. "I'm never going back to segregation," he said. First he went back to San Diego, where he had been stationed. Then he moved to Los Angeles, married, and had a son named Leland. John stayed in Los Angeles until he passed away a few years ago. I wasn't as close to him as I was to Clinton because when I was little, John went to live with our maternal grandmother after her husband died. Clinton, as I mentioned in the previous chapter, went to college on the GI Bill after he left the army, and then he married Myrtis. They had their first child, their daughter Sondera, and he got a good job with the local glass factory, which made windows for cars and trucks.

I had a good time in Shreveport. On the weekends I would hang out with some of the friends that I had gone to high school with, and we would go to the nightclubs in Shreveport. There was also a segregated roller rink, and we'd go there to see the girls. At least twice a week we would ask them out to have a soda or a drink. Many had completed college and were teaching in segregated schools.

During that time I also resumed my relationship with a girl named Marcia, whom I had dated in high school. We dated for about a year before I went to England. She wanted to get married before I left for England, but I didn't want to do that. I would be gone for two years. I didn't think it would be a good idea for either of us.

I worked in the personnel office on base, and one of my duties was to replace the airmen who were returning home after being overseas. Fifteen months into that job, my supervisor, Major George Brown, told me that it was my turn, that I was going to replace someone within a month. He said I had two choices: a three-year assignment in France, Germany, or England; or a one-year assignment in an "undesirable" location such as Korea. I told him I would get back to him in a couple of days. I began discussing my prospects with airmen who had returned from those places, and I also started reading about England and Germany. I also prayed about it. On Monday morning I walked into Major Brown's office and said I wanted to go to England, as close to Heathrow Airport as possible. From discussing possible locations with my friends, I had learned that proximity to the airport was viewed favorably for ease of transportation access. Major Brown agreed and said he would send me to West Drayton, outside Heathrow. He asked, "Why England?" and I said, "Because the language barrier would be less challenging, since they speak English, and it would be easier for me to communicate." Boy, did I have a lot to learn!

I was very excited to be experiencing another part of the world. After saying good-bye to my family and friends, I headed off to be processed in Brooklyn, New York, and then I boarded a boat. Seven days later I arrived in Southampton, England, where I got on a bus to West Drayton. To my surprise, one of the first things I noticed when I got to England was that everything was racially integrated there. I liked it very much. I didn't have to keep "shifting hats," remembering where I was. When I was in the military in Shreveport I lived in two worlds. On base, everything was integrated. Off base, it was a different story, and you had to keep things straight. You didn't want to go into Shreveport and make a mistake by breaking the Jim Crow laws, which mandated racial segregation in all public facilities. I couldn't eat in some places or I'd get beaten up. The environment would be hostile. I had no choice but to adhere, and I hated it. My brother John had a deep-rooted hatred for the South for that very reason.

I really didn't share his feelings toward the entire South, however. I tried to maintain my composure as best I could in the face of adversity. But more than that, I began to wonder how a country like England could function well without segregation and pondered what a peaceful, political solution would look like back home in the United States. I'm not suggesting that England was perfect, by any means. In fact, there were racial tensions and even riots targeting immigrant and minority populations in certain parts of London in the 1950s. But it was while I was stationed in England that I became curious, more keenly aware of and interested in the political process, especially regarding the similarities and differences between the two countries.

Meanwhile, although I was more than four thousand miles away from the Jim Crow laws back home, I did have occasional experiences that reminded me of them. For instance, while I was at Barksdale Air Force Base there was a very light-skinned black airman who could pass for white. When he went off base, he hung around only with black guys because he thought he would be recognized if he tried to pass for a white person. About a year later, when I saw him in England he was passing as white, and he asked me not to say anything—not to blow his cover. He had never tried to pass for a white man in Shreveport, but here he was doing it in England. I would just shake my head in amazement that somebody would want to do something like that. He seemed to be discriminating against his own people. I did, however, honor his wishes and never told anyone.

My supervisor in the education office was Jack J. Sheehan, a white civilian from Rapid City, South Dakota. Our office administered the high school General Equivalency Diploma (GED) exam and coordinated the University of Maryland program in which professors would take a sabbatical from their jobs at the school and come teach on base. Mr. Sheehan wanted me to take care of all the paperwork for that. In addition, my office was responsible for paying tuition for the airmen's children who attended private schools in England.

Mr. Sheehan took an interest in me and encouraged me to get more education. After I had worked with him for three months, he said I should enroll in the University of London and take some evening courses. He also informed me that because I'm black it would benefit me to get a master's degree and then a PhD. "You can do it," he urged me. "It will open a lot of doors for you later." I totally believed him. When he told me this, it reminded me of my early years on the farm when my mom would emphasize the importance of education. So I had Mom, the Bennetts, and now Mr. Sheehan, a white man, all explaining to me the value of education. It helped tremendously because Mr. Sheehan seemed to believe that I was smart, that I could be an asset to society. I think he took a particular interest in me because I was the only black person in the office with a college degree. I was also a hard worker. Whatever job I was assigned to, I would always try to perform it well. Years later I would receive a Christmas card from him, asking how I was doing with my studies.

I really studied hard when I was at the University of London, which meant that sometimes I would have to work at my job on weekends and long into the early morning hours to meet my deadlines to get reports to Washington, DC. For the first time in my life I encountered students from all over the world, including some exceptionally bright students from Africa, even a son of the Nigerian royal family. That surprised me, because back then I was subject to the same stereotypical depictions of Africans as whites in this country were. Africans were typically depicted on television and in books as being not very intelligent—they were always dancing, living in huts, and wearing bones in their noses.

During breaks between classes, a group of British students and I would have tea and talk. Actually, they would talk and I would listen. Because of their accents, their pace of speaking, and the specific words they used, it took me awhile to understand what they were saying. For example, it took me a bit to learn that a *flat* is an apartment, a *subway* is a train, and a *pub* is a bar. I enjoyed the food, particularly fish and chips, and did a lot of sight-seeing. I was excited to see Buckingham Palace, Big Ben, and the Tower Bridge. I was treated very well. We could go wherever we wanted to, with one exception. In West Drayton they had clubs and pubs that catered to different races. Anyone could frequent any place, but one pub would be mostly white and another would be mostly black. In London there was the Douglas House, and it catered to everyone.

The Douglas House, a hotel run by the US Air Force for all US military personnel in London, was in a residential section just off Oxford Circus, very close to Hyde Park and its famous soapbox, Speakers' Corner. Douglas House served as a center of activity for almost all who served in Britain. It had a great bar and good American food, such as hamburgers, hot dogs, and steak. Each military man was allowed to bring a guest. I frequented the club most Sundays while I was in London.

Being stationed in England also gave me the opportunity to travel throughout Europe. I was able to visit France, Germany, Spain, and other countries, where the children of our airmen attended different schools. We also had the benefit of a black man in the communications department on base; his name was William Keyes, and he worked at the switchboard. He became friends with other communications people all over the world. They would normally just chat, but he also began running an informal dating service, providing black airmen at West Drayton the phone numbers of communications women in other countries for the guys to contact when they got there.

Once I had to travel to Madrid, and he gave me the telephone number of a woman to contact there. I had read about the bullfights and was anxious to see one in person. I called her, and she took me to some museums, we ate lunch at a great restaurant, and I did in fact see a bullfight. It was quite an experience seeing people being entertained by this sport. Although my date didn't speak much English and I didn't speak any Spanish, we had dictionaries and were able to communicate fairly well.

In a strange coincidence, I ran into Keyes about ten years ago at a human-rights convention in Charlotte, North Carolina. I heard a guy behind me telling someone else, "I know that guy," and he was pointing at me. To my surprise, it was Keyes! It was great seeing him again. The first thing I said was, "Are you still matchmaking?" We both had a great laugh and caught up with each other's lives.

For fun we would play baseball with other teams in England or take the subway into London to visit friends. It was about a twenty-minute ride and cost about fifteen cents each way. I would often take cigarettes from the post exchange to the English women because they said our cigarettes, which were Lucky Strikes, tasted better than the ones they could get in England. But I could buy only one carton a week because everyone else on base was doing the same thing.

When I was close to being discharged, Mr. Sheehan encouraged me to apply for school at Louisiana State University (LSU) in Baton Rouge, and he helped me with all the paperwork. In the spring of 1956 I was accepted. But then the Louisiana state legislature passed a law that required any individual planning to attend LSU to obtain a letter from his or her high school principal stating that he or she was of good moral character. I went to my former high school principal, Roleith H. Brown (who was black), for my letter of recommendation, and he told me that if he wrote a letter like that he would lose his job. I don't know if someone had threatened him, but I didn't want him to lose his job. I found out later that this was the state's way of keeping black students out of LSU. So I had to apply somewhere else.

I didn't feel good about this at all. And what made it worse was that I had gotten out of the military two months early, in August, so that I could meet school registration deadlines. To add insult to injury, classes had already started at most places, which made it difficult for me to go anywhere else. A friend encouraged me to call Texas College in Tyler. I spoke with the dean and told him about my situation. He informed me that I was applying a week late but that if I got there that day he would let me in. I was appreciative of the opportunity and did everything he asked. I was fortunate that everything worked out, and I was discharged from the air force in 1956.

CHAPTER 4

Back to the Segregated South

~*~

After living an integrated life in England and traveling to cities like Rome, Madrid, and Paris, I knew it would be hard to return to segregation in the South. But I really had no choice, and I figured that I could use my experience in England as a learning tool that could possibly be used to change policies.

Texas College, located in Tyler, Texas, is about ninety miles from my hometown of Shreveport. When I entered the registrar's office, I met my future wife, Joy Green. She was the registrar's secretary, and apparently I did not make a good first impression. I was wearing one of the three suits that had been custom-made for me in England. I was telling another woman in the office that I had just returned from England and that I was going be the best-dressed guy on campus. Apparently Joy was listening and later told me that she thought I was "a little too arrogant."

To my surprise, the graduate students and the staff at Texas College ate in the same area of the dining room. So at lunch I made sure that I sat at the same table as Joy. I quickly introduced myself and asked her, "Where are you from?" She said, "Caldwell, Texas." Then I asked about her family, and she said, "My dad works at a dry cleaner's and alters clothes. He is the best-dressed man in town." No doubt she said this in reference to my earlier proclamation. We had a good laugh and still do, to this day!

One day, Dean Allen C. Hancock, the number two person in charge at Texas College, invited me into his office. He wanted to talk about my experience in education. He began by asking me to work part-time for him about four hours a day, and I eagerly accepted. The job would provide additional income, allow me to demonstrate initiative within the power structure of the college. and allow me to see Joy, because her office was right next door.

Joy had recently graduated from Huston-Tillotson College in Austin, Texas, but she couldn't get a teaching job because there were no job openings at the time. She really caught my eye and made going to work each day something to look forward to. After a few lunches and dinners together, I asked Joy to go to the movies with me. We began dating in the fall of 1956.

Things were going well for me. I had met Joy, I had the GI Bill paying for my education, and I had a part-time job in the dean's office. I enjoyed being able to wear a suit to work daily and was fortunate enough to buy my first car, a 1950 Pontiac.

About once a month I would travel back to Shreveport to spend the weekend with Mom and Dad. I would also take my old girlfriend, Marcia, to the movies. But after I met Joy, my feelings for Marcia were not the same as before I left for England. Joy knew about Marcia, but she never really dwelled on it until she saw me talking to Marcia after a football game at Texas College (Marcia had graduated from Texas College). Joy arrived with three of her girlfriends, who stared me down. I kept talking to Marcia. Later, when she left to go back with her family to Shreveport, I knew I had to commit to a relationship with Joy. I called her and told her, "Let's go for a ride." We went for dessert, and at that time she gave me an ultimatum. She said, "You're going to have to make up your mind between the two of us." I knew then and there that I was going to have to make a decision. In my heart, I knew Joy was the one for me. She was, and to this day she remains my heart and soul, my best friend.

My schedule was very busy. I was in school full-time completing my master's program in education and working part-time. My coursework included the supervision of instruction, the principalship, school and community relations, and the philosophy of education.

In addition to working at my part-time job, I occasionally taught the dean's social-studies class at his request. On the spur of the moment he would tell me, "I want you to teach my class today." Sometimes I would have only a few minutes to prepare for a one-hour class. It normally went well, until one day I ran out of material and couldn't fill the full hour. I dismissed the class early, then went back to the office and saw that one of the students, a graduate art teacher, was complaining to the dean that I had let the class out early. Since the student herself was already a teacher, she was not happy with me as a fill-in. I decided I would never let a class out early again. The next day the dean made sure he taught his class. He didn't stop me from teaching, but he did give me more time to prepare lectures. Occasionally I would discuss my experiences in England, including the country's educational and political systems. I would even tell some old war stories.

In the spring of 1957, time was running out for me under the GI Bill. I was scheduled to complete my master's degree in August and had to get busy finding a teaching job. I wanted to stay close to Tyler, Texas, because of Joy. However, my brother John wanted me to come teach in Los Angeles. My former supervisor, Mr. Sheehan, referred me for a teaching job in Wisconsin, and that school made me an offer. I submitted applications for jobs in a number of school districts closer to home, but no one contacted me. By then summer school was over, and I was becoming anxious.

One day the registrar at Texas College, Eugene Long, received a telegram from the principal of Douglas High School in Sherman, Texas. Mrs. Long knew that I was looking for a job, so she asked me if I wanted to interview for the position. I wasn't sure whether my old car would even make the 150-mile drive, but I said yes anyway.

I set out early in the morning, winding my way through the small towns of Lindale and Greenville and into Sherman. The principal, Mr. Persley Nebitt, greeted me at the school and spent about thirty minutes interviewing me. Then he said, "Come ride with me." I didn't know what that was all about, but we drove to the central office. Months later he told me he had taken me there so that he could compare my application to the others that were on file. Two hours later he told me that I had the job and that I would be teaching social studies.

Then he took me to meet Minnie Johnson, his next-door neighbor. He wanted me to room with her, which I agreed to do. Mrs. Minnie was an elderly woman who needed the money, and she was a good cook. She made breakfast and dinner for me each weekday, and I ate lunch at school. I was really appreciative of the opportunity and very happy to get the job. It allowed me to stay close to Joy.

By the time I left Sherman that first day, it was almost dark. On the way back to Tyler I had car trouble. When I got to Lindale, about thirty miles from Tyler, my water pump started to leak. I got water at a filling station, drove very slowly, and made it home. Joy was waiting for me, and I gave her the good news. About two weeks before school started, I drove back to Sherman and moved my things into Mrs. Minnie's house.

In addition to being a teacher, I also became an assistant football coach. I was approached by the head football coach, Albert B. Gates, to help him. There wasn't much else to do right after school, and it provided some additional income, so I agreed. I was a running-back coach, and my group was pretty fast. The team would play area schools in addition to traveling to Dallas and Fort Worth. That first year we had five wins and five losses. We would have won more games, but our star quarterback was injured midway through the season, and we didn't adjust to his absence very well.

The school was segregated, which I was not happy about. I told myself, "If I can make it through one year here, I am going west." Once during football practice I noticed that the pads that the boys wore under their pants to protect their legs were old, and I suggested to Mr. Nebitt that the players needed new pads. He told me that we had to wait for the white high school to pass their used pads down to us, that we never purchased *new* pads. We also got other hand-me-downs from the white school, like football jerseys. As frustrating as it was, I decided not to say anything.

Adding to my frustration was the fact that I was away from Joy. Because there were so many other black teachers also looking for jobs at the time, Joy stayed at Texas College because she was still having difficulty finding a good teaching position.

For additional money I also worked as a high school basketball referee. After teaching all day, I would go to other towns in the area to officiate, like Paris, McKinney, Sulphur Springs, Mount Pleasant, Bonhan, and Mount Vernon. They were all within a one-hundred-mile radius of Sherman. One night after a game in Paris I had a flat tire on my way home. The jack didn't work, so I slept in my car on the side of the road. Early the next morning I flagged down a farmer to help me change the tire. I got back into Sherman just in time to teach my first class.

The next week, while officiating at a game in McKinney, I made a bad call and almost got run out of town. Unbeknownst to me, one of the rules had been changed in the game. When the score was tied, I gave the ball to the wrong team. What saved me was that the team I gave the ball to missed its last shot, and the home team made two free throws and won the game. That job was tougher than it appeared. I have a lot of respect for game officials, and to this day when I am watching sports I give officials the benefit of the doubt on close calls.

Besides my teaching, coaching, and officiating, there wasn't much going on for me in Sherman. I would occasionally travel to Dallas on weekends to see my uncle, Thomas Ansley (my mother's brother), who had cancer. But most of all I wanted to go back to Tyler to be with Joy.

During the 1957 Christmas season, I went home to visit my family. I really missed Joy. One evening while we were talking on the phone, I said, "I love and miss you and don't want to live without you." Since that day we have been together!

In the spring of 1958 Joy came to Sherman for a weekend to pick out an engagement ring. We visited a Zales store downtown and had fun selecting a ring. Later Joy met Mr. Nebitt and then looked up some of her old friends. We visited them and had a great time. After that weekend we became virtually inseparable. I drove to Tyler almost every weekend to visit Joy.

When school let out, I went to Shreveport for a few weeks. Joy was attending summer school at Prairie View College, taking courses to prepare to be an elementary school teacher. She was also preparing for our wedding. In the meantime, Texas College contacted me and told me that the town of Rule, Texas (about thirty miles north of Abilene), wanted to hire two teachers for a black school. Joy and I traveled there for interviews. We were offered a contract for the 1958–1959 school year. It was only a two-teacher school, so we would have been the only teachers.

We talked about it on the way back and decided not to take the jobs, because I had already accepted a teaching position on the Navajo reservation in New Mexico. We had gone for the interviews in Rule because Joy did not have a teaching position secured on the reservation, but nevertheless we believed that a change of scenery from Texas would be good.

On July 26, 1958, Joy and I were married in her hometown, Caldwell, Texas. My family drove over from Shreveport, and Clinton was my best man.

Joy and I spent our wedding night in Waco, Texas. The next day, Sunday, we returned to Caldwell, packed up our things, and headed for Gallup, New Mexico, about nine hundred miles away. Joy's dad had given me a shotgun and told me to "protect my little girl."

We were excited to go to New Mexico. It was a whole new concept for us. I didn't know anything about Native Americans or Navajo culture, but I said, "Hey, let's try it." I had prayed a lot and sensed that God was trying to show me different things. I always liked to try new experiences.

Driving that distance and all night was a new experience for me, too. We left at 10:00 p.m. that Sunday, driving slowly because we were pulling a U-Haul trailer. We made our way to Abilene, where we filled up our gas tank, at 3:00 a.m. Then through heavy rain we passed Lubbock, Texas, and eventually stopped in Clovis, New Mexico, where we ate breakfast. Through Nat King Cole and others we had heard much about Route 66, and we were anxious to connect with it at Santa Rosa. We reached Albuquerque by noon and ate lunch there. What a beautiful city, Joy and I observed, especially the mountain view. Joy then excitedly announced, "Only 137 miles to go!" and around 3:00 p.m. we finally arrived in Gallup. What a trip! We got a hotel room right across the street from where we were to report the next morning.

CHAPTER 5

My First Teaching Jobs on Indian Reservations

ᴍ

*Y*á*át'ééh* (YAH-te-hay), a Navajo greeting, became an important part of my vocabulary after Joy and I moved west. Who would have thought a Louisiana farm boy would ever be living on an Indian reservation speaking Navajo? Surprising as it may have been, it was one of the best experiences of my life.

Having made the approximately nine-hundred-mile drive from Caldwell, Texas, to Gallup, New Mexico, in nineteen hours, Joy and I were anxious to see what this new opportunity would bring us.

How did I receive a job offer to teach in Gallup? During the mid-1950s, the National Association for the Advancement of Colored People (NAACP) actively encouraged the Bureau of Indian Affairs (BIA) to hire black teachers as a way to support Dr. Martin Luther King Jr.'s dream of integration. Gallup had an NAACP chapter, and it was able to encourage the local BIA chapter to offer teaching positions to black educators.

I had become aware of Dr. King during the 1955–1956 Montgomery Bus Boycott, which was organized after Rosa Parks was arrested on a bus in Montgomery, Alabama, for refusing to give up her seat to a white man. Although I was in London at the time, I was made aware of this event by family members and friends. I was hopeful and eager to see whether the strategy of nonviolence would work in ending racial segregation in Montgomery. I was pleased that it did work—racial segregation ended on all Montgomery public buses. When Joy and I moved to Gallup, Dr. King and others had just recently formed the Southern Christian Leadership Conference, a group designed to conduct nonviolent protests in an effort to achieve civil rights.

The day after we arrived in Gallup I went over to the BIA office to receive my teaching assignment. The BIA ordered me to report to its substation in Fort Defiance, Arizona. This meant I had about thirty more miles of driving to do.

The BIA oversaw a number of Native American boarding schools in New Mexico and Arizona, and I was assigned to teach fourth, fifth, and sixth grades at the Kinlichee School about twenty miles east of Fort Defiance. Native American parents would send their children to boarding schools during the week because most of the parents did not have cars. Thus it was too hard to get their children to and from school every day. So the students stayed in the boarding schools during the week and went home to live with their parents on the weekend. This was all too familiar to me, because it was exactly what I had experienced in Louisiana as a child.

I was glad to finally arrive at Kinlichee. It was a different environment from what I had been accustomed to, not only physically but also culturally. The girls wore long dresses, many of the boys had ponytails, and some of the children wore moccasins. Most of my older students spoke English fairly well, but some of the students in the lower grades only spoke Navajo. It reminded me of when I visited Spain and was challenged by the language. Because of the language barrier, the younger students and I mostly greeted each other when interacting by saying, "*Yáʼátʼééh.*"

Everyone treated Joy and me well. I can't remember a single racial slur or act of discrimination. We were probably the first black people some of them had ever seen. I'll never forget one of my students. His name was Ben Yazzie because he was from the Yazzie Clan, and he would periodically come up to my desk in class, smile, put his hand next to mine, and say, "You're the same color that I am." I would nod my head and verbally agree. I realized it was his way of bonding with me. I always liked talking to Ben. Many of the Native American students were quiet and shy, but he always had something to say. He liked to tell me about what he and the other kids had done the night before, such as playing games or watching movies. Regarding movies, I found it ironic that when some of the Native kids watched westerns, they'd root for the white men to ultimately win. In their eyes the whites were the good guys and the Indians were the bad guys. The only exception was Tonto; since he rode with the Lone Ranger, they said he was okay.

Then there were the living arrangements. The job at Kinlichee came with free housing: a small old trailer parked near the school. We didn't like it. It had one bedroom, a kitchen with running water, and no air conditioning. I had never lived in a trailer before, and I made a vow then and there never to live in one again. The school principal, Charles Sonntag, lived nearby in a three-bedroom house.

The very first night I was there, about five local men drove up and knocked on the door. Joy and I were already asleep. The men wanted to know where the "yei be chi" dance was being held. When Joy heard their voices she told me to go get the shotgun. I thought, "I've got to get rid of these guys." So I told them I didn't know where the dance was, and I directed them to Mr. Sonntag's house next door. To say Mr. Sonntag was not amused would be an understatement. The next morning he sternly asked me, "Why did you send those guys over to my house in the middle of the night?" I told him, "I didn't know where the dance was. I thought maybe you would know." After a moment of silence he smiled and shook his head, and we had a good laugh. Mr. Sonntag and I became very good friends.

I almost went back to my old job in Sherman, Texas. Joy and I were having a hard time adjusting to the environment. We had been in Kinlichee for only a few days, and I was afraid that I had made a big mistake by moving to the Navajo reservation, especially since Joy didn't have a job.

All the new teachers went to a workshop close to Tuba City, Arizona, for a week before school started. Joy was allowed to go even though she was not one of the teachers. The instructor spoke mostly in Navajo. This was done so that we would realize how our students would feel when we spoke only in English. Some of them would not understand us.

When I got back to Kinlichee, I called my former boss, Mr. Nebitt, and asked him if he had already replaced me. He replied, "No, not yet. But are you sure you want to come back?" He advised me to discuss this with my wife and call back Monday.

I talked it over with Joy, we prayed about it, and she concluded that we should stay. She added, "If we go back, we will never leave that place. You don't want that." Joy was afraid that if I went back to Sherman, I might never try anything new again. Wisely, she added, "Let's stick it out for a year and see how it goes." That was the best advice she could have given me. We stayed for the year and never regretted it.

Getting an education was important to the Navajos. This was reflected in the fact that their children were well behaved and respectful. Although there were no formal parent-teacher conferences, Mr. Sonntag advised me to be ready to talk to the parents when they picked up their children each Friday for the weekend.

Saturday was always a big day for the teachers on the reservation. It was our time to relax, and we all would travel to Gallup to shop and visit friends. Sometimes I would run into an old classmate from college who also was teaching on the reservation or into someone I used to know in Shreveport. One of the great friends I made was Fred Houston, a black businessman who ran a shoeshine shop on Main Street. He was president of the NAACP in Gallup, and I would visit him every Saturday. He was very straightforward and would give me advice. We maintained our friendship for years, even after I moved to Albuquerque.

In October Joy moved to Fort Defiance to take a full-time job with the BIA as the local administrator's assistant. That meant that we had to live apart again. Then in January 1959 Joy received her first teaching position at Crystal Elementary School, a boarding school about sixty miles from Kinlichee. There she taught the first and second grades and really enjoyed it. But with a perpetual passion I really missed having Joy by my side.

In March 1959 I was in the shoeshine shop visiting Fred. He told me that he and the NAACP had met with Bernie Caton, the new school superintendent in Gallup, a few days earlier and encouraged him to hire more black teachers and staff. Fred advised me to make an appointment for an interview. He added that there was only one black teacher in the Gallup-McKinley County School District at the time. Thus, the following Tuesday I took leave from work and went to see Mr. Caton. I arrived early, before he came to work. The secretary asked me if I had an appointment, and I told her that I did not. Superintendent Caton arrived and promptly invited me into his office. He spent more than thirty minutes talking to me, during which time I told him my story. I also told him that my wife was teaching miles away and that we saw each other only on weekends.

Mr. Caton was very interested in the fact that I had served in the air force and that I had worked at the air force education office in London. All the while I knew that my job was to convince him that Joy and I were the best teachers he could find, regardless of race. Mr. Caton then instructed me to bring Joy to meet with Chester Portifield, the assistant superintendent.

On Saturday morning Dr. Portifield offered jobs to Joy and me. Mr. Caton had instructed him to hire us and to get Joy certified to teach elementary school (Joy was certified to teach at the secondary level; the Crystal Elementary School on the Navajo reservation was a BIA school and didn't require certification). That summer Joy attended Highlands University in Las Vegas, New Mexico, to take the necessary coursework to become certified at the elementary level.

Meanwhile, I left Kinlichee to attend North Texas University in Denton, Texas. In August 1959 Joy and I reported to Zuni Pueblo, New Mexico (thirty-seven miles south of Gallup), to begin work for the Gallup-McKinley County School District.

I taught fourth grade, and Joy taught first grade. We were finally able to live together again. There were more than twenty teachers in the apartment complex, and for many of them it was their first experience teaching Native Americans. Most of them spoke well of the Zuni students, but there was one exception. One teacher from Oklahoma always talked down to them, telling them how "dumb" they were. It disturbed me greatly, but I couldn't do too much about it because her husband was the principal, so unfortunately she continued to work there.

However, overall I was really happy with that job. It was just as my mom had said: "Education will help you go places." As an added benefit, Zuni Pueblo had trading posts where one could get almost everything one needed. And what the trading posts didn't have, Gallup did, such as fresh steaks and ribs and a Safeway supermarket.

For entertainment, some of us joined a bowling team and drove the thirty-seven miles to Gallup every Monday night to play in a league. Occasionally the art teacher at our school even offered free art classes to teachers in the evenings. Joy would laugh at some of the artwork I would create, such as pictures of houses and the landscape. The paintings weren't very good, but they were colorful and fun to do.

Some of the male teachers formed a basketball team, which I joined. We played once a week, mostly in Gallup, but sometimes we traveled to Window Rock, Arizona, which was about sixty miles from Zuni. One player was the star; he really carried us, night in and night out. He had played college basketball in Oklahoma and was a very good shooter.

Just as I had done in Texas and at Fort Defiance, I officiated basketball games for the Gallup-McKinley County School District. Most games were in Gallup, but I occasionally called games in Grants and Ramah, a mostly Mormon town. Similar to what had happened at a game in Texas, I made an incorrect call and was almost run out of town. Again the home team ended up winning. Call me lucky, I guess!

A year later a couple of television stations from Albuquerque installed a broadcast receiving tower on one of the nearby mountains, which meant that everyone could now receive a television signal. We were excited about that. Since I knew something about installing televisions from my military days, the word spread quickly throughout the community, and our neighbors asked me to install their antennas. I never took the money they offered, so instead they brought me food and sometimes gifts, such as handmade rugs and jewelry. Every Saturday I would climb up on people's roofs and install seven or more antennas. To this day I still have some of the gifts they so graciously provided.

A couple of years later I realized that if I still wanted to take advantage of the GI Bill to go to school, I had to start working on my doctorate again. Thus, two and a half years after we had arrived at Zuni Pueblo I took time off in the spring semester of 1962 to attend the University of New Mexico. I spent many long hours studying at the university's Zimmerman Library. Meanwhile, Joy stayed in Zuni to teach. Thus, for many months I attended the University of New Mexico during the week and drove back to Zuni for the weekend. Indeed, I was an overextended, much-traveled husband and student looking forward to graduation.

CHAPTER 6

Albuquerque

$\sim$

In the spring of 1962 I became a full-time student at the University of New Mexico. In the summer Joy finally joined me, and I no longer had to commute back to Zuni on weekends to be with her. Joy and I really enjoyed Albuquerque. I told her that I could spend the rest of my life here. In fact, we have now lived here for more than fifty years.

When we first arrived, we rented a one-bedroom house. I told the owner that we would live there only for the summer because we were going to be schoolteachers for the Albuquerque Public School District and were waiting for our assignments. She understood and then asked the neighbors on each side of the house if they would have any problem living next to a black family—there were no other black residents in the area. I didn't know that she was going to ask that question, but it relieved me that I was only going to be there for the summer. Apparently everything was okay, because we moved in right away.

In late August we received our teaching assignments. I was assigned to Lincoln Junior High School, and Joy would be teaching at Lowell Elementary School. We quickly went to see the schools, which were both located in the Southeast Heights, very close to each other. That was important to us, because we only had one car.

After visiting the schools, we began looking for a house in the nearby area. We drove around looking for houses for sale, and we found three that we thought we might like. All were brick and were located just north of the airport. As soon as we got home, we called Brown Realty to make an appointment to see the houses. A young man there told us he would pick us up at 9:00 a.m. the next day. He said he was happy that we called and that he looked forward to showing us the houses.

Meeting him was a different story. When he arrived and I opened the door, the first thing he said was, "Good morning. You all are Negroes." I replied, "All of our lives." Then he said, "We sold those three houses," and I responded, "Overnight?" He began to tell me about other houses that he could show me, all of which were in black neighborhoods.

Growing up in segregated Louisiana, I always knew in the back of my mind that I would meet people who were prejudiced, so I understood where he was coming from. But the houses he wanted to show me were undesirable to me. One was on the 5300 block of Candelaria Northeast, an area that became known for blockbusting, the practice of inducing white homeowners to hastily sell their homes at a low rate, even at a loss, by claiming that the arrival of black (or other minority-group) families in the neighborhood would depress property values; then the homes would be resold to other white people at an inflated price. I knew about two black families who had moved onto that block, and I knew that there were three homes for sale. I didn't want to go to an area from which whites were fleeing. I didn't want to run whites out of their neighborhoods.

Other houses the realtor wanted to show us were in the area known as the Kirtland Addition. It had been all white at one time but was now predominantly black and Hispanic. Given my positive experiences living in an integrated military environment, in integrated London, and with Native Americans, and the fact that Dr. King was leading an effort to integrate society, Joy and I wanted to live in a more integrated community. We thanked the realtor for coming over, and he quickly left.

Joy and I were taken aback by our encounter with the realtor. In Zuni everyone had done everything together. All the teachers socialized with one another, went bowling, ate meals, and went to church together. We never expected segregation to happen in Albuquerque.

Joy and I talked about the situation over lunch and decided to visit the same area again. This time we would look for homes for sale by the owner. I thought that at least this way we might have a better chance of meeting an owner who wouldn't turn us away. So we finished eating and decided to go out again.

We found three homes that we wanted to look at, so we called the owners and made appointments for the next Monday night. I made sure to tell them on the phone that "we are Negro teachers."

All the owners were very friendly. However, when we came out of the first house, there were about a dozen people standing on the sidewalk looking at us as though we were from another planet. They were the neighbors. No one said anything to us or tried to block our way, but it was obvious that they were thinking, "Who are these people coming to our neighborhood?"

When we came out of the second house, we saw that another crowd had gathered, and then one man asked me, "Why do you want to live in this neighborhood?" I didn't respond, and we quickly drove away. I didn't want to get him and his neighbors riled up. The homeowner was at the door, and they were angry at him, too. I told Joy that I didn't think we would want to live on that street.

The owner of the third house, a stucco home at 2900 Hyder Southeast, was very nice. He was a professor at the University of New Mexico. After some discussion about my assuming his Federal Housing Administration loan and the amount we would have to pay him, we reached an agreement. Two days later we owned our first home, and there had been no angry neighbors outside. Joy and I felt good about our decision.

We had only one weekend to move in, because on the following Monday we had to report for teachers' orientation, so we rented a U-Haul trailer, drove to Zuni (where we had left some things in storage), picked up the rest of our belongings, and came back. I thanked the principal there for letting us store our things for the summer. He wished us good luck in Albuquerque, and we invited him to visit us when he and his wife came to town.

On Monday morning all the new teachers met with the superintendent and his staff. After the meeting we were divided into small groups, then we boarded buses and were driven around town to meet the business community. It was just something that people did back then at the start of a school year. We went to the banks and the other major businesses in the area. Joy and I were the only black individuals on our bus, and everyone treated us well.

Things didn't go as well at home, though. After we moved, people started littering our lawn with garbage at night, including watermelon rinds and beer cans. This happened several times. Frustrated, I thought, "What are these people trying to do to us?" I talked to a neighbor across the street, and he was angry about it, too. My next-door neighbors on one side never said a word to us for two or three years. And then there were the prank telephone calls (hang ups late at night). This occurred for a couple of weeks in an effort to prevent us from staying in the neighborhood. I even heard there was a plan to buy my house (I didn't know about that until years later).

Fortunately, a state-district judge named John B. McManus Jr. lived just one block away and heard about what was going on in the neighborhood. He decided to address the issue and called the US attorney general's office, which sent an agent out to the neighborhood. The federal agent went door-to-door and asked all the neighbors if they were part of a movement to get us to move out. Everyone he spoke with denied having anything to do with it. After that, however, we didn't have any more problems.

Years later Judge McManus became chief justice of the New Mexico Supreme Court. I thanked him for what he had done for us back then, and we became friends. Once I became a state legislator, during the legislative sessions he would invite me and other legislators to his home in Santa Fe for dinner. I looked forward to these occasions.

Joy and I were very pleased with our home. It was a medium-size house, with a large living room and two bedrooms, a den that was a converted garage, and a large backyard. We spent most of our time watching television and reading in the den. We developed friendships with several families in the neighborhood: the Romero, Fritz, Todd, Hill, and Christie families.

We also enjoyed our teaching assignments. Joy taught fourth grade at Lowell Elementary School, and I taught seventh-grade social studies at Lincoln Junior High School. I really liked teaching my students—they were eager and interested in learning. I would take Joy to work early in the morning and pick her up in the afternoon.

In late September Joy and I decided to join a church, so we visited some black churches and some white churches. We prayed about it and believed the Lord was calling us to the First Baptist Church of Albuquerque. At that time it was the largest Baptist church in town. It was also all white.

One Sunday Joy and I attended the morning service and filled out a visitation slip asking for a visit from the pastor. On Tuesday William Wyatt and one of his assistants came to our home. They did not know we were black until they got there. We told them that we planned to come to church next Sunday and join the congregation.

Later I learned that when Dr. Wyatt returned to his office he called an emergency deacons' meeting. Apparently they had a long discussion about the two black people (us) who planned to join the church. Hosier Benton Horn, the deacon chairman, was very supportive, but there were other deacons who didn't want us to join. That Sunday, when the vote was taken on whether to admit us as members, there were some no votes, but not enough to keep us from joining. That was fifty-two years ago, and we are still active members of the church today, where I serve as an elected vice chairman of deacons and Joy is a Sunday school teacher. Several years later, when I was the principal of La Mesa Elementary School, Dr. Wyatt called and asked me to hire his daughter as a teacher, which I gladly did. It just goes to show how people and times have changed.

In 1963 Joy gave birth to our son, Lenton Jr., or Lenny, as Joy nicknamed him. He was born on September 11 at Presbyterian Hospital. He was due on September 30, which is my birthday, but on September 10 Joy and I were at a social gathering when her water broke. We drove home to pick up her things and then took her to the hospital. But Lenny wasn't ready to be born yet. The nurses prepared Joy for labor for about three hours, and at about 1:30 a.m. the doctor finally told me to go home and get some sleep. So I went home, but two hours later the telephone rang. It was the hospital, telling me, "We think she's ready." I jumped up, got dressed, and rushed out of the house. The doctor and I arrived at the hospital at the same time. He told me, "You just wait here in the lobby. I'll see what I can do." Less than an hour later, he called me upstairs to see my "big bouncing boy."

I was so proud, thrilled, and happy. My primary caretaking responsibility was to get up during the night and change Lenny's diapers. That was my specialty. But one time I accidentally stuck the diaper pin into his skin, and he certainly let me know about it!

Lenny was a good baby and slept quite a bit. He was up only once a night. We had been trying to have a baby for quite a few years, so when God finally answered our prayers, we were overjoyed.

Like many kids, including myself, Lenny enjoyed watching and playing sports. I installed a basketball hoop in the backyard, and whenever we watched a game together on television, he would go outside at halftime and mimic what he had just seen. At times I had difficulty determining what was more entertaining to watch, him or the second half of the game on television. He would do the same with football games. I always got a kick out of that. He would throw the football and then run after it to retrieve it. He was only about three or four years old at the time. He also enjoyed playing with Lincoln Logs and Legos; he would erect very creative buildings, houses, and stadiums.

Since Joy and I were educators, we really focused on Lenny's educational development, starting at an early age. We knew he was smart, but we were a bit concerned that he was the only black student at his elementary school, Bandelier. He performed well as a student, and if he experienced any racial incidents he didn't share them with us. He then attended Wilson Middle School and Highland High School, where he was a starter on the football team (freshman year) and the basketball team. He also ran track and was recruited by several area colleges.

Lenny earned a bachelor's degree in economics from the University of New Mexico. Joy and I were encouraging him to continue his education and get a master's degree, so one day he approached me with a proposition. He said, "Dad, I'll go back to school and get my MPA [master of public administration] if you will help with my tuition." He had been working full-time as a city land-use planner, but because of budget cuts the city was planning layoffs. I answered, jokingly, "What's in it for me?" He responded, "Your Christmas and birthday gifts to me won't have to be as extravagant." We both laughed, and of course I said yes. He received his master's degree in public administration, then proceeded to work in Las Cruces as a planner. Three years later he joined the city of Rio Rancho as a planner, then held a similar position for the city of Albuquerque. In 2002 he volunteered for the gubernatorial campaign of former US secretary of energy Bill Richardson. After winning the election, Governor Richardson asked Lenny to serve in his administration; first he named him the deputy secretary of labor, and later the state workforce development director in the Higher Education Department. After the Richardson administration ended, Lenny began working for the

UNM Health Sciences Center as the College of Nursing student services manager, where he provided policy work.

I love my son—he's my angel. He never gave Joy and me any problems. One reason he's always been able to stay out of trouble, I believe, is that he has always been attracted to team athletics and has benefited from the structure it provided and the positive influence of his peers. Also important is his Christian faith, which his mom and I have been instrumental in shaping. Today he plays on several city and travel tournament basketball teams and attends Calvary Chapel. I've always believed that it is easier to avoid mischief if you surround yourself with people doing positive things.

When I later became the principal of John Marshall Elementary School in Albuquerque, I would watch the kids during their lunch break; they would eat lunch and then have forty minutes until class began. During this idle time, some students would begin arguing about petty things, and this would occasionally result in fighting. The kids just had too much time on their hands. So I asked the physical education teacher to organize some games. That ended the arguing and fighting. The students just needed to stay busy.

I tried to keep busy as well. I was in bowling leagues, I learned to play golf, and I worked out at a gym six days a week, but never on Sunday. When I was at home I did yard work and, as I like to say, other duties assigned by my wife.

In 1963 I continued to take evening classes at the University of New Mexico—two each semester. During that summer I took two or three classes. By 1964 I had received my master's degree and was halfway done with my doctoral work. At that time I didn't know that the superintendent of the school district was considering me for a promotion, but it didn't take long for me to get the message.

In October 1964 my professional life took a pivotal positive turn. One day, while I was in class teaching, the school principal came into my classroom and told me that the Albuquerque Public Schools (APS) superintendent wanted to see me. I went to his office and he told me, "I want to make you the first black principal at APS. Do you think you can handle the job?" Of course I answered, "Yes, sir." It may have paled in comparison to Jackie Robinson breaking the baseball color line in 1947, but I understood the significance and was excited!

He said, "I am going to send you to John Marshall Elementary School, but

I want you to get out from behind the desk, get into the community, and visit with the pastors and all the business leaders in the neighborhoods." Not only was this job significant in terms of title, it also provided me with additional resources. The promotion enabled Joy and me to purchase a second car.

When I began my new job, I noticed the schoolchildren were eating lunch at their desks. The meals were cooked in the central kitchen and bused in. It was a little unsettling to me and reminded me of when I had to eat lunch at my schoolhouse when I attended grade school. I didn't like that, because it made the day seem to go by more slowly. I believed that the students needed a break from the classroom to eat and socialize, and then they should return to the classroom. This period of relaxation would allow them to refocus when they returned and would maintain the classroom as a learning environment.

I met with the superintendent, Charles Spain, in an effort to secure resources for a cafeteria. He indicated that the request had to be approved by the school board to be placed on the next year's bond issue with other school-capital projects. The request to be included in the bond election, about five months away, was approved. In the meantime, Dr. Spain instructed me to gather community support for the measure.

I was certainly energized to begin the process. I reached out to a local pastor in the area and met with business owners and residents. The bond passed, much to the delight of the community and, most important, the schoolchildren. I felt as though I'd won my first election.

I stayed at John Marshall for three years, but during the 1967–1968 school year I worked part-time because it was the University of New Mexico's policy that if you were completing your PhD you could not work full-time. The school superintendent allowed me to work at APS headquarters as a student counselor during that period. I needed only two more classes to finish the doctoral program and write my dissertation, which was entitled, "Aspirations of Anglo, Spanish, and Negro High School Students."

Through my travels and experiences with educational systems, I developed an interest in the aspirations of students of color. By working in the educational office in the air force and teaching in Texas and on the Indian reservations, I had observed white as well as minority students. In some cases I observed a difference between the ambitions of minority students and those of white students: sometimes the ambitions were lower among the nonwhite students. I wanted to study this further. I found that a considerable amount of research existed on the aspirations of adolescents in general, particularly for white students, but not so much for students of color (predominantly Hispanic and black students). There was some research on socioeconomic class and aspiration and a bit of research on ethnicity and aspiration, but not specifically a comparison of white and nonwhite students. So I set out to compare the educational and occupational aspirations of the white, black, and Hispanic students.

I tested students in the ninth grade at several schools and asked them what they were interested in doing when they graduated from high school. I also tested students in the twelfth grade and asked them the same question, and for most of this group I discovered that their goals had changed since ninth grade. Among all ethnic groups, the aspiration to work in higher-level occupations increased. There was a difference, however, between the male and female students' aspirations. For example, Hispanic female students saw themselves working in lower-level, secretarial positions; the rate of this occurrence was followed by black and then white female students. Among the male students, however, there was little or no difference in the occupational aspiration level. In addition, I discovered that a significantly higher percentage of white students had attended a private kindergarten. At that time there was no kindergarten offered in the public school system. Thus, I basically found that the disparity in the aspirational level between white and minority students was related to social class. On the average, the students of color tested at a lower level than the white students.

Joy and I graduated from the University of New Mexico in June 1968. She received her master's degree and I received my PhD on the same day. I still have the newspaper article written about the event. Apparently the media thought it was newsworthy that we graduated together. My mother and father, as well as my two older brothers and their families, were sitting in the audience when I walked across the stage. I was the first one in my family to receive a bachelor's degree and a PhD as well. After I received my PhD, the superintendent promoted me to principal of La Mesa Elementary School, a larger school in the Northeast Heights.

Despite my professional advancement, my social life wasn't very good. Joy and I weren't welcome at the nicer clubs in town. We tried to go to dances and have fun, but we were often turned away because we were black. So one evening Joy and I and a group of black professionals went as a group to one of those places, and the manager let us in. That seemed to break the ice, and we never had any problems like that again. None of this really surprised me, though. This was the mid-1960s, and it was only a couple years earlier that we had experienced the housing discrimination.

Soon I became involved in politics. In 1965 I started attending the precinct and ward meetings at Bandelier Elementary School. In 1966 I was elected one of the delegates to the state convention—I was the only black delegate from my ward. At the convention I got to know Governor Jack Campbell and many other elected officials.

CHAPTER 7

The Transition to State Politics

I n the late 1950s New Mexico fared well in educational performance compared to other states, and it also did better then compared to how we perform currently. At that time public education was funded through a state gross-receipts (i.e., sales) tax. That changed when John Burroughs was elected governor in 1958. A peanut farmer from Portales, New Mexico, Burroughs began working to eliminate earmark funding for specific programs. Public education was a target and began to suffer a decrease in revenue. We had only one educator in the state legislature then, Representative Fred Foster from Deming, New Mexico. He was a teacher and served on the House Education Committee. He did a great job, but he was only 1 out of 112 legislators. In an effort to combat the imbalance, a group of educators to which I belonged decided to strategically increase the number of legislators with educational backgrounds.

Our educational group consisted of teachers, principals, college professors, and graduate students from all over the state. Representative Foster spoke at our meeting and strongly encouraged us to get into politics. He advised us to support campaigns that had an educational focus and run our own candidates with educational backgrounds, especially from our own areas. We met several times during 1965 and 1966, typically at the University of New Mexico, and in 1966 we ran our initial group of candidates.

While I was still working on my PhD, I was approached to run. I was hesitant, but I decided this was not about me as much as it was for the educational team. I, along with several others, decided to run for office. I ran for the state senate.

Until 1966 New Mexico had thirty-two senators, one representing each of the thirty-two counties. There was only one senator for each county, regardless of population. As the result of a federal lawsuit, a judge ruled that a reapportionment was necessary, and this provided several of the larger-populated counties more than one senator. Bernalillo County, where I lived, would now have ten senators. I decided that this would be an opportune time for me to run, but I faced several challenges. First, a large portion of the newly created district was located in the South Broadway and South Valley areas, and only a small portion included the Southeast Heights, where I lived. Second, the judge's ruling was made in March 1965, only a couple of months before the June primary. Although I worked very hard on the phone bank and on door-to-door campaigning, I really had very little name recognition. There were five candidates in all, and the winner was Thomas Benavides. Thomas was a great guy, and I eventually became good friends with him.

Of the six education-focused candidates who ran that year throughout the state, all were defeated except Benito Chavez, a junior high school principal in Espanola. Although most of the candidates lost, we did learn a lot about the political process.

In 1968 the group again approached me to run for office, this time for the state house of representatives. Again I was very hesitant because of the challenges. I pointed out that I was a black man living in a 99 percent white district and that the incumbent legislator was a Republican while I was a Democrat. But the group insisted that I run. After praying and seriously contemplating, I agreed. I thought that I could bring a different perspective to the educational agenda. Having recently acquired my PhD, I believed that I could bring a voice to those who were less fortunate and had challenges accessing our public educational system and performing well in it. I would address these challenges, which were based on several factors, including socioeconomic level and race.

In early 1968 we held our initial campaign-planning meeting at my home. Most of the individuals who attended were part of our education group, but there were also a few neighbors. One of those individuals was Ben Raskob. I was very fortunate to have his support. Ben had relocated to Albuquerque from New York; he lived about two blocks from me and was a very influential millionaire. He had converted from Judaism to Catholicism and was a generous donor to St. Charles Catholic Church.

Another supporter was Desi Baca, the principal at Riverview Elementary School. He owned several apartments and offices in town and offered one of his unoccupied offices to me at no charge for my campaign headquarters. Rita Raskob, Ben's wife, cleaned the office and had three telephone lines installed. She volunteered to coordinate the telephone bank on my behalf. The Raskob sons also helped by putting up campaign signs in the area and going door-to-door passing out my campaign literature. I was pleasantly surprised and very grateful.

My campaign team wasn't very formal. I had eager help from fellow college students and educators, who made many phone calls and campaigned door-to-door in the spring and summer of 1968. I went to at least four hundred houses several times.

I won the primary in June. I had only two opponents this time, and not many people voted during the primaries. I also campaigned pretty hard. But the general election in November was another story. I was set to run against Ed Dunn, who was a white Republican in a predominantly white Republican district.

I recruited about forty volunteers, again including educators and students, to work on the campaign. Many of them would meet every Saturday morning at my house for coffee, doughnuts, and fruit before going door-to-door. Joy's sorority, Delta Sigma Theta, donated $400 to my campaign. We used it to buy nine thousand bumper stickers, yard signs, and campaign brochures.

My campaign workers and I spent quite a bit of time going door-to-door again, passing out leaflets, and talking up my campaign. Unbeknownst to me, Ben held a campaign fund-raising party at his home that summer but didn't invite me. He wasn't being disrespectful, nor was he a racist, since he was obviously supporting me. I believe he was simply cognizant of those who might be hesitant to support me because of my race. I was told he invited about one hundred very influential people, including judges, city councilors, attorneys, and prominent residents of the Southeast Heights and the Ridgecrest area in particular. Ben was doing quite a bit of work behind the scenes, telling people that he wanted to help elect the first black state representative: me, Lenton Malry. Ben apparently spent some of the money he raised to conduct polls on my electability. Looking back, I can't help but draw a bit of a parallel between presidential candidate Barack Obama getting his boost from the Iowa caucuses, in a predominantly white state, and me receiving support from a predominantly white legislative district in 1968.

During this campaign I was the principal of La Mesa Elementary School. During the summer, when I wasn't at work, I was knocking on doors. I probably knocked two or three different times on every one of those four hundred or more doors in the twelve precincts that made up my district. Most of the time I was treated well and received positive feedback, but some neighbors were not so nice. They would give me a mean look, and some would say, "*You* are running to be our state representative?" I would say, "Yes, I am." Others would just reply, "Okay," after I introduced myself; they wouldn't indicate whether they were going to support me.

Then there was one neighbor, Ted White, who was blatantly racist and rude. When he saw me coming up his walkway with my campaign literature, he would stand behind his screen door and coldly state, "I don't let niggers come to my front door." It surprised and upset me, but I would think of Dr. King and his mantra of nonviolence and simply nod my head and walk to the next house. Years later, when I was campaigning for reelection, I even returned to Mr. White's house to distribute campaign literature. Lo and behold, he didn't call me names! But in keeping with his racist beliefs, he told me, "I hope you don't vote for that dago Pete Domenici or that communist George McGovern." What a character.

When I was campaigning for the fourth time, in 1974, Mr. White not only took my literature but also asked me to put one of my campaign signs in his yard! I think about Mr. White from time to time and remember him eventually telling me that he and his wife were going to vote for me. In six years I went from being called a nigger to being addressed as Dr. Malry. This proves to me that people truly can change.

When I was going door-to-door that summer, many people asked me to come into their homes, but I never did unless I really knew them. I was concerned that someone would twist the situation around and say I did something bad to them. I didn't want any trouble. It was just part of what I dealt with sometimes. A year earlier a candidate had been falsely charged with harassing a woman in her home. I didn't want to take any chances.

I was creative in my advertising. On my campaign signs I utilized my professional title, calling myself Dr. Lenton Malry instead of simply Lenton Malry. Many voters didn't know what kind of doctor I was. Sometimes they would ask me what area of medicine I specialized in, and I would tell them that I'm not a medical doctor—that my PhD was in education.

I enjoyed campaigning door-to-door. I began to "read" people—I could sense whether they were going to vote for me. I loved talking to people. I think I got that from my mom. She was really outgoing and she was an avid talker. Talking to people also provided me with an understanding of some of the issues people were concerned with. But there was a downside to door-to-door campaigning as well. Several hours of walking certainly provided exercise, but it also caused my feet to hurt. I quickly learned to wear two pairs of socks for extra support every time I went out.

In November 1968 I was elected with 56 percent of the vote, and I became the first black state representative in New Mexico. On election night Ben Raskob invited me and my family over for a steak dinner. I was nervous about the election results, but I accepted the invitation anyway. We ate, and the polls closed at 7:00 p.m. By 7:30 I was naturally very anxious to find out the results. Ben calmly informed me that I had won. When I said, "What?" he replied, "We had a[n exit] poll taken, and you won. You won by a fairly decent margin." All I could say was "Wow!"

That sounded good, but I wanted to be sure. So I went to Bandelier Elementary School (which was two blocks away), because that's where six of the twelve voting boxes were supposed to be. When I got there, at about 8:00 p.m., Ed Dunn, my opponent, was already there checking the results. He came out right away, shook my hand, and said, "Congratulations, you won the election." And I had indeed won the votes in the six boxes. But there were still six boxes uncounted. Three of them were at Highland High School, and I knew that the farther east one went in the district, the more conservative or Republican it became. So I thought I would go to just one more place and find out how I had done there.

When I got to Highland, I couldn't believe what happened next. An election worker held up a sheet with the results as I walked in and said with a smile, "You won all the boxes here. Congratulations!"

I went back to Ben's house, picked up Joy and Lenny, and hustled home. It was one of the happiest moments of my life. I called a lot of my family and friends. Several friends came over and celebrated until about 2:00 a.m. I then got a few hours of sleep, woke up, and went to work the next day. Everybody at work was happy for me too.

It turned out that I got 2,753 votes to Dunn's 2,167. I had never referred to my race in the campaign. I just talked to people about my ideas to support quality education, and I found out that many people didn't mind paying higher taxes if the taxes were fair and were used for something good.

By winning the 1968 election for state representative for District 18, I made history. Ed Meacher, a reporter from the *Los Angeles Times*, heard about the story and contacted me the next day. He was in New Mexico covering the Reies Tijerina story at the Tierra Amarillo Courthouse in Rio Arriba County in the northern part of the state. Tijerina, who was originally from Texas, led a struggle in the 1960s and 1970s to restore New Mexican land grants to the descendants of their Spanish colonial and Mexican owners. He made international headlines when he led an armed raid on the Tierra Amarilla Courthouse in 1967.

Mr. Meacher called me the day after my election and asked me for a political interview, so I met with him for about an hour in my office at La Mesa Elementary School. On November 28, 1968, my story appeared in the *Los Angeles Times*—I didn't even know that it had appeared until my brother John called me from Los Angeles and said, "What are you doing in my paper?" I was excited about it and surprised that my election was such a big story. I asked John to send me some copies, which he did.

The article quoted me as saying that my attitude was the "key" to getting elected. "You must believe in yourself," Mr. Meacher quoted me. "You can't tell yourself it's no use doing a good job because they're going to discriminate against you. After that, and most important, you've got to be able to get along with people."

For the next few years our political group continued to run educators for the legislature. Don Thompson, a teacher, was elected to the state senate, and Abel McBride, the assistant principal of West Mesa High School, also got elected. We ended up with about nine or ten individuals in the legislature, and I truly believe we made a difference. In the mid-1970s we were able to give the teachers an 11 percent salary raise, and I led the charge to give the University of New Mexico $10 million to upgrade its library. I served in the New Mexico legislature for ten years, from 1969 through 1978.

Looking back on those years, I feel good about breaking the color line. I believe that in some small way it gave young black children hope that they could achieve their dreams. In fact, I remember Eddie Corley Jr., currently a prominent car dealer, telling me that as a teenager he used to watch me on television when I was a state representative. He said it made him believe he had a real chance to make it in life. And he did: he became a state representative in Grants, New Mexico, for four successful years. I feel very good about being a positive role model, and I wonder how many other black people were motivated by seeing me on television.

During my ten years in the state legislature I was on the House Education Committee and served as its chairman for six of those years. I enjoyed the opportunity to work with all the university and college presidents in the state and almost all of the 89 superintendents of public education.

CHAPTER 8

Reflections on Serving in
the New Mexico Legislature

⌒ℳ⌒

I never could have predicted my first day in the New Mexico House of Representatives.

I was in my office at the Roundhouse, where the legislature meets, when a young man came running down the hall, yelling, "Doctor, doctor, come quick! One of the secretaries has fainted."

I went to the bathroom, got several wet paper towels, and put them on her face. Thank goodness she was up and around in about a minute. I wondered whether there had been anyone else who could have helped. Evidently someone had informed the young man to "get Dr. Malry down here fast." I quickly recalled my campaign signs that had referenced me as "Dr. Lenton Malry." My fellow legislators all had a good laugh and occasionally teased me after that about practicing medicine without a license.

That was the third Tuesday in January 1969, which meant, according to the New Mexico Constitution, that the legislature had to convene. But before the session each party met and selected its leaders. We Democrats elected David Novell, an attorney from Clovis, speaker; George Fettinger, an attorney from Alamogordo, majority leader; and Severino Martinez, a general contractor from Espanola, majority whip. Then the party decided on the committee assignments. I was given two very good assignments: the Education Committee and the Appropriations and Finance Committee.

I had campaigned on an education platform and was eager to get started with policy making in that area. In the two months before the beginning of the legislative session, I attended many meetings and social events sponsored by the leaders of the Albuquerque Public School District, the University of New Mexico, and the city of Albuquerque. Each of these groups wanted additional financial resources that only the state legislature could provide. So it became pretty obvious that if I wanted to positively affect educational policy, financial resources were a critical component.

Since the public schools were heavily dependent on state funding, I met with APS Superintendent Charles Spain. One of my priorities was to ensure access to quality education for minority students. We discussed several areas to address, one of which was capital projects. I also met with representatives of the National Education Association—the teachers union—which was seeking additional funding. After that meeting I introduced a bill allowing sabbatical leave for public school teachers, and it passed in February 1969.

Not all my efforts centered on education, however; I also helped provide resources for economic development. The city of Albuquerque wanted support in the form of a 2 percent hotel- and motel-room tax to finance a $9.2 million convention center for Albuquerque. City Commission Chairman Pete Domenici said the bill would allow Albuquerque and other nearby cities to use the tax for economic development. The Appropriations and Finance Committee passed the legislation because Albuquerque's population was growing, and many similar-size cities had convention centers. Many citizens of Albuquerque agreed that a convention center would be good for attracting conferences and promoting tourism in the area.

I am also proud to have authored two other bills that passed: House Bill 240, which gave consumers the right to see their credit bureau ratings for free, and House Bill 195, which provided two additional district judges for Bernalillo County. The latter bill lessened court congestion and provided speedier legal decisions. In my first two years as chairman of the Education Committee, I passed more bills than any other freshman legislator. I really listened to constituents and acted on what I believed were much-needed pieces of legislation.

In January 1971 there was a big shift in the leadership of the New Mexico House of Representatives. David Novell, our speaker, became the state's attorney general. That left the speaker's position open, and there were two men who really wanted it: George Fettinger, our majority leader, and Walter Martinez, an attorney from Grants and the chairman of the Judiciary Committee.

Each of the candidates came to my home asking for my support. Each also offered me the vice chairmanship of the Education Committee. I decided to give my vote to Martinez because I wanted to fill the speaker's position with someone from the northern part of the state. Furthermore, I believed I could progress more quickly under Martinez. The night before the big election for Speaker of the House, all the legislators met in Santa Fe. The first vote was a tie, 24–24. The second time around Martinez picked up three votes and won, 27–21.

We also elected David Salman, a rancher from the northern part of the state, majority leader and Abel McBride, the assistant principal of West Mesa High School, majority whip.

Thus, when the 1971 legislative session began, what was called the Mama Lucy Gang was in charge: a team of mostly liberal legislators, some of whom had gone to Highlands University in Las Vegas. Mama Lucy was a woman who operated a local café. She was a gracious lady who gave free meals to anyone who couldn't afford to pay. Because of her kind heart, we named our team after her.

During my first two-year term in the legislature, I chose to sit in the back row of the chamber because I had two friends from Albuquerque who sat there, and it was easier for me to observe the other legislators and the process from that vantage point. But in 1971, at the start of my second term, I moved to the second row and stayed there for the next eight years. Salman, the majority leader, helped me on many occasions, including by giving me an aisle seat and then allowing me to move up to the second row, which I really appreciated.

In the summer of 1971 the house leadership named me the chairman of the Drug Abuse Interim Committee. Interim committees met when the legislature was not in regular session, so we held meetings once a month all around the state. There was a lot of interest then (as now) in addressing drug abuse. We gathered information about the problem from educators, law-enforcement officers, mayors, and concerned private citizens. I was particularly concerned about drugs in our schools. At that time marijuana was the most popular drug among students, and I took a personal interest in the subject because one of my neighbors had a significant drug problem that was ruining his life.

In January 1971 our interim committee wrote the first drug-abuse bill in

New Mexico's history. The bill required drug-abuse education for all seventh graders, and I viewed it as an early warning system to lessen the threat of drug use in our state. I had been in the legislature for only two years and was very happy to be part of the leadership for change. After the drug-abuse bill passed, the committee disbanded in 1972. I was then selected for and named the chairman of the Health and Aging Committee. Thus, at the time, I served on three committees: Health and Aging, Education, and Appropriations and Finance.

In January 1973, at the start of my third term, I was named the chairman of the Education Committee. This meant that my primary focus had to include not only K–12 initiatives but higher education as well. This is when I authored what I considered the most important bill in the legislature, House Bill 360.

House Bill 360 mandated statewide kindergarten for all five-year-olds by 1977. Consistent with my platform of quality access to education, I strongly believed that every child should have access to early childhood education no matter where he or she lived. These are the formative, foundational years in a child's life. Lower-income children had Title I assistance, and upper-income children could attend private schools, but middle-income children didn't have any financial support. New Mexico was one of only two states that had no early childhood education. I had introduced the bill every year for three years but couldn't get it passed. Once I was chairman of the Education Committee, however, I had more power to influence. I also had the support of the house leadership.

The only real challenge I had was from Aubrey Dunn Sr., the chairman of the Senate Finance Committee. I took him to lunch at the Bull Ring (a local watering hole for legislators and "movers and shakers") to talk about the bill after it had passed the house and was now before the senate. He told me, "I like you, but I don't like your babysitting bill." I knew then and there that I couldn't change his mind, but I asked him not to speak against the bill when it was introduced on the floor. He didn't give me a firm answer, but when the bill came up for a vote, he got up and walked out of the chamber. That was the best thing that could have happened. The bill passed the senate by three or four votes, and many people consider it one of the most important pieces of legislation ever passed in New Mexico. If Dunn had spoken against it, it would have died. It was a watershed moment for me when Governor Bruce King signed the bill into law, and I became more popular in the legislature. (A side note: Senator Dunn's son, Aubrey Jr., was elected state land commissioner in 2014.)

One of my closest friends in the legislature was Representative John Radosevich. We sat next to each other and shared the same microphone. One day I was speaking on the floor of the chamber, trying to get a bill passed to create a sickle-cell anemia citizens group to distribute information throughout the state about a disease that primarily affects black people. This was a public preventative health measure; however, some of the legislators didn't see it that way. They were concerned that I was introducing legislation that would benefit only one race of people. John, frustrated from listening to the dissenting narrative, took the microphone from me and put a dollar bill on the table and said, "Let's get Representative Malry treated and forget about the rest of them." No one raised any more objections, and the bill passed almost unanimously. That's the kind of friend John was.

My close friends were not limited to Democrats. Sitting across the aisle from me was Hoyt Patterson, a Curry County rancher and Republican leader. We didn't vote together on a lot of things, but we were good friends. Having grown up on a farm and a ranch, we could relate well to each other. He would joke, saying, "We're both minorities—you're black, and I'm a Republican in a Democratic-controlled house." I'd get a big laugh out of that.

I also got along well with Governors Dave Cargo, Bruce King, and Jerry Apodaca. Cargo was governor when I was first elected. He was a moderate Republican and just a great guy. I used to go up to his office on the fourth floor and talk to him, primarily about minority issues and education. King was a rancher, a teetotaler, and a Baptist like myself. We often discussed ranching and religious issues. I knew Apodaca because I served with him in the legislature when he was a senator. I got a kick out of him—sometimes literally. We played basketball together to raise money for charity, and his on-court aggression was so great that he would knock other players down just to get the ball.

In 1974 I wrote House Bill 85, which established an equitable funding formula for public education. I thought this was important because it allowed access to quality education to students who lived in rural areas. Having grown up in a rural area with very limited financial resources, I identified with those in New Mexico with similar backgrounds. I knew that one key to my success had been access to quality education. Many of the school districts in these areas, mostly in the northern portion of the state, were not being provided with enough financial resources to be effective, and I believed that legislation was necessary to alleviate this problem.

In 1975 the Democratic leadership gave me another big problem to solve, but it wasn't in education, it was in medicine. The doctors in New Mexico were experiencing large rate increases in their malpractice insurance because the insurance companies were including them in the same category as doctors in Arizona and California, where a growing number of patients were filing medical-malpractice lawsuits. The doctors wanted the Health and Aging Committee, with me as chairman, to come up with a solution to their problem.

We spent all summer studying the issue, and in the next session we introduced four bills, all of which passed and were signed into law. I authored all of them. First, we proposed legislation that would allow New Mexican doctors to set up their own insurance company. This would alleviate the problem.

The second bill called for removing taxes from prescription drugs and any goods and services purchased by a physician's order. In our hearings around the state, we became aware of a growing number of people living on Social Security. We tried to provide them with some financial relief for their prescriptions, because every dollar meant a lot to them.

The third bill called for the establishment and enforcement of more stringent standards to ensure the safety, cleanliness, and operation of nursing homes. The legislature had been receiving a lot of complaints about nursing-home operations. The more we learned about these issues, the more it appeared New Mexico was lagging way behind the rest of the nation. I believe we helped, in some small way, to improve that issue.

Fourth, I became aware of a man who lived in Gallup who had to travel to Albuquerque three times a week to get dialysis. He had to leave home on a bus at 11:00 p.m. to be in Albuquerque the next morning to get on the dialysis machine. I introduced a bill that established dialysis machines in various hospitals throughout the state. It was one of the pieces of legislation of which I was most proud.

After the 1975 legislative session I created a newsletter for my constituents and named it the *Malry-Gram*. Twice a year I sent out about five thousand copies to the voters in my district. It explained how the legislative process worked and what I was accomplishing. It also included any positive media coverage that I received. Each issue was typically about four pages long. Joy would copyedit and proofread it before it was printed. The *Malry-Gram* was a big hit with voters. Many times I was at the grocery store, at church, or at a park and someone would come up to me and say, "I got your *Malry-Gram*. Thanks for sending it." I used it as a way to promote what I was accomplishing and to facilitate feedback and dialogue among my constituents. It seemed to serve these purposes very well.

CHAPTER 9

WICHE

⸺

I n March 1972 Governor Bruce King invited me to his office. He asked me, "What do you know about WICHE?" I told him that I had some knowledge of the organization—that it was the Western Interstate Commission for Higher Education and that its purpose was to facilitate resource sharing among western universities. It had been formed in 1951, according to its charter, to "expand access to high-quality higher education to citizens of the West." The governor informed me that he was going to appoint me to be one of New Mexico's commissioners.

I was elated, because in serving as the chairman of the Education Committee, I was learning about issues facing our colleges and universities. I knew that WICHE was one of the finest and most challenging organizations in higher education, and serving as its commissioner would afford me the opportunity to interact with governors, legislators, and higher-education leaders in all of the western states. I hoped that I could learn about best practices and implement some of them here in New Mexico.

WICHE, a volunteer organization, consisted of representatives from all thirteen western states, a regional grouping that includes Alaska and Hawaii as well as eleven states of the continental United States. New Mexico was, in fact, the first state to join WICHE, on December 19, 1952, an effort led by the UNM president, Tom Popejoy. That was certainly a source of pride for me. The commission was funded through private grants and public resources, and each state had three commission representatives. As the first black person to represent New Mexico, I was keenly interested in how other states addressed minority-student issues, particularly access.

As soon as I joined WICHE I began identifying the influential members and quickly became friends with them: William E. ("Bud") Davis, the president of Idaho State University; Glenn Terrell, the president of Washington State University; and Glenn Dumke, the chancellor of California State University and Colleges, Los Angeles. We seemed to connect very easily. For instance, Dr. Terrell brought some fresh salmon from Washington to a conference in Denver. He had the cook from the hotel prepare the salmon and then invited me and four other friends for dinner. We had a great time. I knew then that I was part of the inner circle of WICHE.

I was a WICHE commissioner for twelve years, from 1972 to 1984, and I was selected to be the vice chairman to Chairman Bud Davis for the 1974–1975 school year. Dr. Davis taught me a lot about WICHE and about higher education in general. The commission had ten subcommittees, and I served on two: the Committee on the Future and the Finance Committee. The other eight committees were Executive, Student Exchange, Economic Development, Health and Human Services, Information Clearinghouse, Minority Education, Investment, and Communications.

In 1974 Dr. Davis applied for the presidency at the University of New Mexico. At our meeting in Las Vegas, Nevada, that year, he gave me his résumé and other credentials and asked that I submit his application to the UNM search committee. I lobbied on his behalf, and he was selected. I hope I helped him.

At our conference in the summer of 1975 in Sun Valley, Idaho, I was chosen to replace Dr. Davis as chairman of the commission, and Dr. Dumke was named to succeed me as vice chairman. I was excited and felt very fortunate. There were articles about it in several New Mexico newspapers, and here is what the Associated Press wrote about it:

> State Rep. Lenton Malry, D-Bernalillo, is the 1975–76 Chairman of the Western Interstate Commission on Higher Education. He is the first New Mexican to hold this position in more than 20 years.
>
> Malry has been vice chairman of WICHE the past year, and succeeds Dr. William E. Davis as chairman. Dr. Davis, who was a delegate from

Idaho and the president of Idaho State University at Pocatello, is the new president of the University of New Mexico. "I'm happy that I can bring this recognition to New Mexico," said Malry. Malry becomes the second New Mexican to serve as Chairman of WICHE since it organized 25 years ago. Dr. Tom L. Popejoy, who was UNM president at the time, serviced as WICHE chairman during 1953–54.

As chairman, Malry will bring next year's annual conference to New Mexico. The conference will be held Aug. 9–13, 1976, in Albuquerque, and Malry said he plans to give the commissioners an opportunity to visit Santa Fe at least one day of the meeting.

Governor King had appointed me to WICHE in 1972, and Governor Apodaca reappointed me in 1976. That year I asked Governor Apodaca to appear as our keynote speaker at our annual conference at the Hilton Hotel in New Mexico. On request I gave the commissioners some free time during the conference for touring, and many of them visited Santa Fe, Old Town, and the Sandia Peak Arial Tramway. I also hosted a party at my home. The commissioners had a great visit to our state.

The annual WICHE conference was always held in the summer, so my family and I always planned our vacation around it. We would usually drive to the conference because I wanted to sight-see and explore the beautiful West. One of our longest vacations was the year the conference was in Seattle. From Albuquerque we drove to Los Angeles to visit my brother John and his family for almost a week, then we drove up the coast to San Francisco and stayed there a couple of nights, and after that we went to Portland, Oregon, for a couple of nights. During the conference we took a ferry over to Victoria, British Columbia, and spent some time there. When the conference was over I packed my ice chest with lots of seafood and we drove back to Albuquerque. We had been gone for more than two weeks and had had a great time seeing the West Coast.

A few years later the conference was in Spokane, Washington. Dr. Terrell invited me and my family to spend a few nights with him and his family at Washington State University in Pullman, which is about one hour from Spokane. Again we took off in the car, this time through the Rocky Mountains. We spent several days visiting Yellowstone and Grand Teton National Parks.

We took a lot of pictures and had a great time. We then continued to Pullman and stayed two nights with Glenn and Francine Turrell. Glenn and I played lots of golf. I remember Francine giving Joy a recipe for buttermilk pancakes that we still use today. They're delicious!

I was learning more and more about higher education in general and the important initiatives that WICHE could institute. Back in New Mexico, while serving as a legislator, I was always responsible for facilitating the progress of the bill that made the appropriations for WICHE. Also, at the request of Dr. Davis, I assisted with the UNM budget. One year he asked me to make an appropriation to upgrade the university library. I got a bill passed that gave $10 million for books, materials, and capital projects for the UNM library. I also sponsored legislation to build a new engineering-department building.

In 1975–1976 I was very busy serving as WICHE chairman. Once a month I would fly to Colorado and spend the night in Denver, then rent a car the next morning and drive to Boulder to meet with the senior staff from 9:00 a.m. to noon. The staff would brief me on policy and administrative activities. At that time we were filling a vacancy for executive director—Dr. Robert H. Kroepsch was retiring. We had had a great working relationship, and I was pleased to be referenced in his outgoing director's message:

> The year 1975 has been an important one for WICHE and for me
> personally. Just to cite a few examples: The Commission elected
> Dr. Lenton Malry as its Chairman. He is a state representative in
> New Mexico and knowledgeable in the ways of government and
> politics. He is also an educator, sensitive to the issues and concerns
> of higher education. But there is more. Lenton Malry is Black and
> the first member of any minority group to be elected to the WICHE
> chairmanship. This speaks of several things: of Lenton Malry himself,
> of the changing times, and of WICHE as a changing organization. The
> membership of the commission has altered since I joined the staff in
> 1960; it is more representative than it was. There are now five minority
> members and seven women.

I created a search committee to fill the position and named Adrian R. Chamberlain, the president of Colorado State University in Fort Collins, the committee head. The search committee also included my vice chairman, Dr. Dumke, and he and I spent many hours on the phone discussing the candidates. After many long hours of interviews, we met in Denver and selected Phillip Sirolkin as the new executive director. He was the executive vice president and the vice president of academic affairs at the State University of New York at Albany. Although he was from the East Coast, he had worked at WICHE in the late 1950s. Dr. Sirolkin was instrumental in developing WICHE's Mental Health Council. He had vast experience in state and federal positions as well as in complex institutions. Dr. Sirolkin served the commission well.

WICHE continued to grow steadily. In 1960 there were only fifteen people on staff, and the budget was less than $400,000. However, by June 1, 1976, there were two hundred people on board, and the budget was $8 million.

Although some of the current initiatives were implemented a few years after I left the commission, we provided some important foundational work that resulted in the development of some of these initiatives. For example, one initiative was the Western Undergraduate Exchange program (WUE).

When I discussed issues of higher education with my constituents, they would give several examples of challenges they faced. A common issue was the out-of-state tuition for programs that didn't exist in New Mexico. This encouraged my continuing focus on accessing quality education. The commission studied and discussed the matter at length, and a few years after I left, WUE was implemented. WUE permits all western states to allow nonresident students to enroll in their state institutions for a lower rate than the out-of-state tuition. The program does not take into consideration the availability of degree programs in the student's state of residence, nor does it consider the student's family income in granting admission. Students who enroll in WUE pay one and a half times the in-state tuition. Therefore, the total tuition a nonresident student pays is greatly reduced. For example, at the University of New Mexico, a WUE student would pay about half the standard nonresident tuition. The annual average savings for a student enrolled in WUE is about $7,500.

WICHE thus provided great opportunities for students who aspired to study in advanced programs, and it was dedicated to enriching the lives of these young people who were striving to think, learn, and serve. I was proud to be part of this mission.

CHAPTER 10

My Last Two Years in the Legislature

⟡

hile the first Concorde commercial
flights were taking off in the United
Kingdom, riots marking the beginning of the end of South African apartheid
were occurring in Soweto, and here in the United States we were celebrating
our two hundredth birthday of independence from British rule. That year,
1976, was a very busy time for me. I was completing my chairmanship of
WICHE, teaching a political-science course at the University of New Mexico,
and working full-time for the Albuquerque Public School District.

I was also running for reelection for my house seat. I was somewhat
surprised that I had a primary-election opponent: Larry Husted, a self-
employed researcher. He graduated from Highland High School and had a
bachelor's degree from the University of New Mexico in political science. I
felt pretty confident about my reelection prospects, so I really didn't spend
much time campaigning in the spring, since most of the constituents in the
district knew me and my work. In March, the *Albuquerque Tribune* published
an article that stated, "Rep. Malry seeks 5th term in House. He said the
legislature completed a funding formula for public schools a few years ago,
and next year must pass a formula for higher education."

In addition, I released a new edition of the *Malry-Gram* that described
the laws I had gotten passed in the 1975–1976 legislative sessions (my fourth
term). The highlight was House Bill 256, Health Facilities Licensing, which
mandated that hospitals and other health facilities be licensed and that their
records be kept confidential.

Frank Hesse, a medical doctor, neighbor, and good friend, was concerned with the quality of health care and wanted to shape health-care policy. He provided me with great innovative ideas, which I took to the legislature for study and ultimately the creation of legislation. One of these ideas became House Bill 256.

During the 1975–1976 sessions, a number of bills in a medical-malpractice package were intended to solve a crisis situation facing New Mexico physicians, who were scheduled to lose their major malpractice-insurance carrier, Travelers Insurance Company, when it left New Mexico on March 1. The legislation allowed doctors to set up their own insurance company. The bill also gave the State Board of Medical Examiners greater authority to restrict, suspend, or revoke a physician's license; to police itself; and to rehabilitate doctors who were discovered to be on drugs.

As a legislator, I really learned to listen to people and to appreciate the input that informed people provided. I took time to read and answer the many letters that constituents would write to me, which was typically several hundred per session. Because I was a member of the House Appropriations and Finance Committee, most of the letter writers were seeking community funding for capital projects such as community centers and Little League fields.

I won the primary fairly easily, and on the next day I caught an early morning flight to Portland, Oregon, where I spoke at a mental-health conference sponsored by WICHE. George Lowe, the associate director of WICHE and the director of the state's Division of Mental Health and Human Services, had invited me to speak. I discussed how New Mexico's mental-health and human-services programs provided the opportunity and served as mechanisms for the western states to discuss and address common mental-health and criminal-justice issues. These issues could best be addressed by pooling state resources and expertise; facilitating cooperation among state mental-health agencies, local service providers, and higher-education programs; and providing technical assistance and staff resources.

I then began focusing on the general election. My opponent was Juan Raigoza, a teacher at Highland High School. In the fall I campaigned door-to-door, as I had always done. Rather than talk about my experience, however, I would just say, "It's that time again." I was certain that more than 90 percent of the people in the district already knew who I was.

Dr. Hesse served as my treasurer, and he and his wife, Zora, went door-to-door campaigning for me as well. They were so valuable and hardworking. One afternoon Zora and I had been walking door-to-door in her neighborhood, passing out my brochures, for nearly two hours. By the time we quit, I was dead tired. After we got back to Zora's house and I was getting ready to leave, she told me, "I'm not happy with the response we got on one street. Let's go back and work it again." I told her I was too tired, but she wouldn't take no for an answer. So we went back and walked around again until dark. I, or should I say *we*, won that precinct!

In November 1976 I was elected to my fifth term in the New Mexico House of Representatives (a term is two years). One of the most debated bills in the next year's legislative session was a joint resolution that would have barred women from becoming members of the cadet corps at the New Mexico Military Institute (NMMI). Forty young women had applied to the NMMI cadet corps in the fall of 1977. Already approved by the state senate, the bill to bar them was defeated in the house by a vote of 37–30. I was very passionate about this legislation; it spoke to my core focus of access to quality education for all. One of the newspapers printed a speech I gave on the house floor just before the final vote:

> New Mexico Military Institute is a good institution. The nine years that I have served in this New Mexico legislature, I have supported their budget, and I hope that I will be able to continue to support their budget. I think the administration and the Board of Regents of N. M. Military Institute is making a mistake. They agreed to accept women into that institution, and then began to proceed to do everything possible to keep women out of that institution. I think that was a big mistake. It puts me in mind of the Little Rock situation back in 1957 when the Governor of the State of Arkansas agreed to admit black students in the Little Rock High School, and then proceeded to pull out the National Guard to keep them from coming in. I think that was the serious mistake on the part of the officials of the New Mexico Military Institute.
>
> Mr. Speaker, it has already been pointed out that this issue has already been taken to the people.
>
> I'm amazed that on March 12, 1977, we are discussing whether to discriminate or segregate in New Mexico. I am amazed when we have made so much progress in eliminating discrimination and that's what the bottom line is . . . whether you like it or not . . . the bottom line is

discrimination at New Mexico Military Institute. That's what we're talking about. My daughter should have the same right to attend NMMI as anyone else. I'm a taxpayer . . . and she should have that right. Any minority sitting here knows that such discrimination has taken place in the United States. Anyone who says they have concern for human rights and human dignity cannot say they are for segregation. They cannot say it.

Mr. Speaker, I have not had a lot of requests, but I do have one from a gentleman who is my neighbor . . . he lives down the street from me . . . his daughter is a senior at Highland High School, and she wishes to attend NMMI. If we pass this resolution, what we're going to be saying is that you as a taxpayer cannot send your daughter to NMMI to take the training that she thinks she would like to take.

Mr. Speaker, and members of this house, I'm appalled at the individuals bringing this resolution before this legislature. This is a slap in the face to everyone who stands for integration and dignity. That's what it is, Mr. Speaker, and I cannot see anyone voting for this type of legislation. It's strictly segregation. I ask the New Mexico Council to look into the year that the New Mexico Military Institute admitted blacks, because I knew that at one time they did not admit blacks. It was not until 1967—ten years ago—that they admitted their first black cadet. Ten years ago, we could have been debating whether to let blacks in. I think it is ridiculous for us to be discussing whether to let females into the Institute.

Someone asked me after they saw the television series *Roots*, "Did people really treat people this way years ago?" and my answer is "Yes, yes, they were treated that way." We kind of look at that now, and it doesn't mean very much to us, but people were really treated that way.

You know, I don't know how many of you have ever been discriminated against, but it's not a good feeling for someone to say to you, "You can't do this . . . You can't go to school here." After I'd served four years in the air force for my country, I came back to Louisiana and I could not be admitted to LSU because I was black. So . . . you don't know how it feels to hear you can't . . . you can't go to this school . . . you can't buy a house here. And that's what we're talking about here. We're talking about segregation . . . at public expense. When I bought the home that I live in . . . in the Southeast Heights of Albuquerque, just in 1962, there was a petition passed around that I couldn't buy that house. I bought it, and I got garbage thrown on my lawn . . . I got crank phone calls . . . but just six years later, they voted for me to represent them in this legislature. Just six years . . . after I'd moved in, and I've been reelected more times than any other previous house member from that area.

So things can work out . . . if we'll just think about it a little bit . . . just think. Things will work out at NMMI. If they admit women, their standards aren't going to go down. They're already recruiting about 60 percent from out of state at the present time. The gentleman from Otero says, "I'm amazed that we even have to vote on this in 1977." We're saying, "Let's have a segregated school at the public's expense." That's what we're saying. That's the bottom line.

After I made that speech, we took a vote, and the bill was defeated by seven votes. It was 10:15 p.m., and several local radio stations had broadcast my speech live.

There were others who provided remarks, but my remarks were arguably more passionate. I was emotional and would not yield the floor until Representative Abel McBride indicated, "We have the votes." It was then— and only then—that I stopped talking!

I was very pleased that we had enough votes to kill the bill, especially since it had already passed in the senate. This was one of the most significant accomplishments in my political career. In the aftermath of the vote, I received several letters from people all over the state, including the neighbor who had a daughter who wanted to attend NMMI. He and his family sincerely thanked me. I believe that this is what I was sent to the legislature for, to be a positive agent for change.

My focus was on the integration of and access to quality education. Initially I mostly focused on minority issues, but as I spoke with more of my constituents, I became more informed about sex discrimination and disability issues, and these also became a staple of my platform.

I introduced several pieces of legislation in that session, and the following house bills (HBs) were passed in 1977:

HB 65, Property Taxes Payment Dates
HB 117, Health Insurance Policies
HB 121, Bernalillo County Medical Center Neonatal Unit

HB 123, Board of Education Finance Exempt Salaries

HB 249, University of New Mexico Mechanical Engineering Department

HB 328, Legislative Retirement Eligibility

HB 459, Neglected Child Defined

HB 460, Child Abuse Reporting Duty

House Joint Memorial 16, Memorial for Dr. Tom Wiley

The following legislation passed in the house and became law in 1978:

HB 25, State Library Deposit Distribution System

HB 26, Computer Library Data System

HB 54, Street Improvement Fund

HB 55, Public Purchases Act Definitions

House Memorial 2, Secretaries Achievement Study

Before the end of the 1978 legislative session I began traveling around the state speaking to different groups about education and other community-related issues. I had received positive feedback about my service as a legislator, and several groups asked me to speak to them. With my legislative experience, the contacts and friendships I had forged, and my involvement with WICHE, I wondered whether a run for lieutenant governor might be possible.

I visited with some high school seniors in Alamogordo and met with the local NAACP chapter in Clovis. I was informed ahead of time that twenty people were expected to attend, but because the president of the chapter was of town, only five people showed up. I was not very happy, to say the least. There was one pleasant surprise, however: a white couple I had taught with at Zuni Pueblo attended. It was great seeing them again and catching up.

Even though I had not yet formally announced my candidacy, I wanted to get my name out in different communities and gauge the response, But driving two hundred miles to speak with only five people was not a good use of resources. Driving back to Albuquerque, I wondered, "Do I really want to run for lieutenant governor?" New Mexico is a large state, and I knew it would be a challenge to reach all the communities to campaign in person, never mind raising enough money to fund a campaign. I spent hours contemplating that question.

My parents, Mary and Peter Malry, married sixty-nine years

My graduation, Central High School, Shreveport, Louisiana, 1948

My grandmother, Leah Ansley, 1938

Me as a freshman, Grambling College,
Grambling, Louisiana, 1948

With Tom Davies, US Air
Force, West Drayton, England,
1955

In the US Air Force, 1955

Joy and me on our first date, at Texas College, Tyler, Texas, 1956

My first teaching job, where I was also a coach, at Douglas High School, Sherman, Texas, 1957

Our wedding day, July 26, 1958

In Window Rock, Arizona, 1959

With my brother John, 1959

My first day as the principal of John Marshall Elementary School, Albuquerque, 1964

Joy and me, featured in the *Albuquerque Journal*, 1968 (courtesy of the *Albuquerque Journal*)

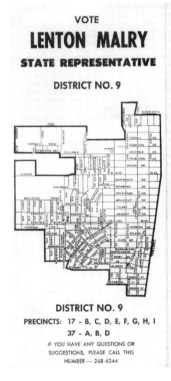

VOTE

LENTON MALRY

STATE REPRESENTATIVE

DISTRICT NO. 9

DISTRICT NO. 9

PRECINCTS: 17 - B, C, D, E, F, G, H, I
37 - A, B, D
IF YOU HAVE ANY QUESTIONS OR
SUGGESTIONS, PLEASE CALL THIS
NUMBER — 268-6344

Give Me A Chance . . .

TO REPRESENT YOU

LENTON MALRY

DEMOCRAT FOR

State Representative

DISTRICT NINE

VOTE   VOTE   VOTE   VOTE   VOTE

Campaign brochure for my election as state representative, District 18 (formerly District 9), 1968

My first day as a state representative, Santa Fe, New Mexico, 1969

Meeting with University of New Mexico students, 1970 (courtesy of the *Albuquerque Journal*)

DISCUSS ISSUES: State Reps. Lenton Malry, left, and John Radosevich, both D-Bernalillo, discuss several of the bills facing New Mexico legislators as the current 60-day session nears an end. The two lawmakers and their colleagues in both the Senate and House are facing a multitude of issues, with only four days remaining to settle the disputes.

(Journal Photo)

Reviewing legislation with my good friend Representative John Radosovich, 1972 (courtesy of the *Albuquerque Journal*)

With my good friend and
office mate, Representative
Roberto Mondragon, 1973

Governor Bruce
King signing my
most significant
piece of legislation,
the Statewide Kin-
dergarten Act, 1973

With the University of New Mexico's President William E. Davis, discussing legislation to fund the Zimmerman Library (courtesy of the Albuquerque Tribune)

Ribbon cutting for the neonatal unit that I helped pass legislation for in 1976, with a woman named Mrs. Martinez and her daughter, who had been a patient in the unit

Joy and me, 1976

With Otis Echols and Crystal Gayle at the New Mexico State Fair, 1977

Weekend work at the legislature, Santa Fe, New Mexico, 1978 (courtesy of the *Santa Fe New Mexican*)

Campaigning for lieutenant governor in Lovington, New Mexico, 1978 (courtesy of the *Lovington Leader*)

CHAPTER 11

Running for Lieutenant Governor

◦◦◦

After serving ten years in the state legislature, I wanted to serve a larger constituency and develop policies that would affect the state as a whole. I spent many hours contemplating a run for a statewide office, and this turned into days and even weeks. Then finally, in the summer of 1977, I decided to run for lieutenant governor. One of the major concerns I had about running was the need to raise significant financial resources, which meant that I would have to travel around the state frequently for fund-raising events. In addition, I knew that being black would be a significant hurdle, but I figured I would simply work extremely hard introducing myself and explaining my platform, which I believed would resonate with the electorate regardless of race.

Joy and Lenny indicated that they would support me in whatever decision I made, but I was mostly motivated by two friends of mine who, like me, had sought to become the first black lieutenant governors in their states: George Brown from Colorado, and Mervyn Dymally from California. They had both been state senators before running successfully for lieutenant governor in 1974. I met them at a national conference for black elected officials and developed friendships with them. When I told them about my decision to run, they asked, "How progressive a state is New Mexico?" I replied, "I don't know, but one way to find out is to run."

I then assembled my campaign team, led by manager Gayle Doyle, and we developed our strategy. My platform emphasized education, health care, and senior citizens. I would tout my experience in each area, consisting of the legislation I had introduced and passed as well as my work experience. For each speech I wrote, I created five-, fifteen-, and twenty-minute versions so I could adapt to varying time constraints. I also adjusted each speech to fit the location and the audience I spoke to.

I was fortunate that several newspapers from around the state did stories on my candidacy. The *Las Cruces Sun-News* led the way by announcing my candidacy on Thursday, August 25, 1977: "State representative Lenton Malry, D-Bernalillo, has announced his plans to unveil his Lieutenant Governor campaign this Saturday."

I made the official announcement at the Four Seasons Motor Inn in Albuquerque. The *Albuquerque Journal* covered the event and published the following:

Malry to Seek Lt. Gov. Spot

Citing his qualifications, State Rep. Lenton Malry, an Albuquerque school administrator, announced Saturday he will seek the Democratic nomination for lieutenant governor in the 1978 primaries.

"I believe I am the best qualified person to seek the office," the 45-year-old Malry told a crowd of supporters at the Four Seasons Motor Inn.

Malry cited among his qualifications his long association with education in New Mexico, his five terms in the House, where he is Chairman of the Education Committee, and major pieces of legislation he has authored.

A number of officials from Albuquerque Public Schools and the University of New Mexico, where Malry earned a doctorate degree, were on hand for the formal announcement.

Malry is the equal opportunity officer for the Albuquerque schools, where he has been a teacher, school principal, and cultural awareness program director.

Introducing Malry was Dr. Chester Travelstead, retired provost at UNM. In the audience was Dr. William E. Davis, President of UNM.

Malry told the crowd of more than 300 that if elected, he would serve full-time as lieutenant governor and sever his connections with Albuquerque schools. The legislature made the office full-time in 1970 with a $15,000 a year salary. In the last session, the legislature increased the lieutenant governor's salary to $30,000 a year.

"I see the role of lieutenant governor as an expanded one," Malry said. "I can work through the Governor's Service Centers to help people solve problems. I can work with the governor and the business community through the Department of Development to encourage development of clean industry in the state to provide jobs. The lieutenant governor, working with the governor, can help streamline governmental agencies and committees to help ensure efficient use of our tax money. I also see the lieutenant governor as one of the governor's chief advisors."

He noted his statewide kindergarten bill, which passed in 1973, as "the legislation I am most proud of." Other major pieces of legislation Malry sponsored included medical malpractice bills for practitioners, the purchase of dialysis machines for kidney patients in the state, and the introduction of a neonatal unit at Bernalillo County Medical Center.

As Chairman of the Interim Legislative Committee on Health and Aging, Malry noted he was instrumental in extending tax credits for senior citizens. As lieutenant governor, Malry said he would support another tax reduction "if the state surplus funds stay near $100 million."

Born in Shreveport, Louisiana, Malry earned a bachelor's degree from Grambling University and a master's degree from Texas College.

His wife, Joy, and son, Len, were in the audience when Malry announced.

Rich Sims, who sought the Democratic senatorial nomination, is the only other candidate to formally announce so far for the nomination of lieutenant governor.

Others who joined the race were Senator Gladys Hansen from Las Cruces, Senator Tom Rutherford from Albuquerque, Senator Otis Echols from Clovis, and businessman Roberto Mondragon from northern New Mexico. All were good candidates and even better people.

Reactions to my announcement were mostly positive. Ten years of service in the state legislature provided me with a track record for voters to review. Passing key legislation on issues that all citizens could benefit from minimized the race factor—well, most of the time.

At my first campaign rally in Hobbs, which was attended by a large crowd, I handed out my campaign brochures and spoke for a few minutes. Before I had finished, a guy in the audience yelled, "Who is that nigger up there?" Everyone got really quiet, but I kept talking as though I hadn't heard a word. I didn't fear for my safety, because I believed he was simply expressing his ignorance and nothing more. He didn't harass me again after that. I had come to expect some of that sentiment while campaigning—just not so quickly!

That negative encounter was balanced out by many positive ones. During the fall of 1977 I spoke to a group of senior citizens at Highland Community Center in Albuquerque, and as I was leaving, an elderly white woman approached me and squeezed a five-dollar bill into my hand. Looking intently at me, she said, "I sure want you to win. I believe in your message." She was so sincere. She visited the community center practically every day and was living on Social Security. Whenever I would tire from campaigning or become discouraged, I would think of her and her belief in me, and it would fuel my desire to continue. I never heard from her again, but that simple act of generosity stayed with me forever.

I campaigned very hard. I traveled around the state speaking and holding fund-raisers. We raised about $75,000 in all. My largest contribution was from my old friend Ben Raskob, who gave $5,000 to the campaign, and my smallest was the $5 from the elderly lady at the Highland Community Center.

I met weekly with my campaign manager and team to discuss the events of the past week and to plan for the weeks ahead. Our strategies included the development of platform planks, such as a brochure detailing my legislative success in health and education initiatives. The newsletter *Lenton Malry for Health—for Education—for New Mexico* publicized key pieces of legislation I had been instrumental in passing and included pictures of me with my family, Governor King, and other constituents. We also attended many campaign rallies around the state and enlisted supporters to engage in as many local media interviews as possible. I utilized every contact I had with educators and community-service organizations, such as the Kiwanis Club, to get things accomplished. I did a lot of radio and newspaper interviews. I would call the news directors and editors to see if I could talk to them about my campaign, and they would usually give me five minutes on the radio at no cost. In most cases I was able to get a newspaper interview as well on that visit.

My second campaign rally in Hobbs, on January 13, 1977, went significantly better than the first. I was honored by the Lovington Democratic Women's Club, first at a coffee reception at Liberty National Bank in the morning, and then I addressed the women at a luncheon at the Pioneer Steak House in the afternoon. I touted my record on education, as usual, but also emphasized my success on health initiatives, particularly those that affected women's health. The luncheon was well attended, with approximately sixty people in the audience. It was one of the best welcomes I had received. The crowd was enthusiastic and supportive. It felt like Lenton Malry Day in Lea County.

Louise Ward, the president of the Lovington Democratic Women's Club, was the one who had invited me. I had met her in Santa Fe a year earlier when she came to the legislature to lobby for funding for libraries and education. Between the coffee reception and the luncheon she was nice enough to take me to the local radio station for a thirty-minute interview. That was the longest broadcast interview I had done up to that point. After the luncheon I thanked everyone and headed to Clovis for a rally the next day.

It was another large campaign rally, but I wasn't the only speaker. There were other candidates running for other offices, and each got five minutes to speak. Afterward I went through the crowd and shook a lot of hands, saying, "I appreciate you coming out" and "I sure would like to have your support." I don't remember anyone not shaking my hand. I was feeling pretty good about my campaign. The next day, a Saturday, I drove to Fort Sumner to speak at a Democratic rally, and this too went very well. There was a large, enthusiastic crowd that seemed very supportive. Of course, just when you think you're riding high, life has a way of bringing you back down to earth.

Later that night, about 8:00 or 9:00 p.m., when I was driving home, one of the belts on my car broke between Fort Sumner and Santa Rosa. I was driving an old Mercedes, and I heard something just go *pop*. I stopped at a service station in Santa Rosa, and the attendant advised me to take a chance and drive the 116 miles I had left to go to Albuquerque. In the back of my mind I thought he just must not have the belt that I needed, but I took his advice and, praying all the way, fortunately made it home by 1:00 a.m. In retrospect, I realize it was a pretty big risk and could have turned out to be dangerous.

Then I developed a case of laryngitis. I went to the doctor, who said, "There's not much I can do for you. Try not to speak, and drink a lot of fluids."

You'll never know how hard that was for me to do! I was out of commission for about one week.

I was invited back to Hobbs for a third rally, and it also went well. I had an event in Carlsbad the next night, so I tried to get an event planned for that day. I called a state representative I knew in Eunice, about twenty miles south of Hobbs, and spoke with his wife to ask her if she could invite a few people for me to talk to that day. She said, "Give me until noon." I had no idea what to expect. She told me to meet her at a certain drugstore, which is where I would be speaking, and when I got there, there were almost sixty people waiting to hear me talk! That was one of the most pleasant surprises I had during my campaign. Who would have thought that sixty people would show up in predominantly white Eunice, New Mexico, to listen to a black man running for the second-highest office in the state? But they were more concerned about who would address their issues—like education, taxes, and jobs—than they were about race.

After spending two hours in Eunice, I went on to Carlsbad, where I was met with a big sign out in front of the Holiday Inn that read WELCOME TO CANDIDATE FOR LT. GOV. LENTON MALRY. When I checked in, the concierge said everything was on the house. I didn't know until later that the owner was Willard C. Kruger of Albuquerque. He was a great man I felt privileged to know. That night about a hundred enthusiastic supporters attended.

Our campaign strategy consisted of an early focus on Albuquerque and the eastern portion of the state, but I did travel to other areas. One of my last campaign appearances was in May 1978 in Las Vegas, New Mexico, to meet with a professor and group of students from Highlands University. After I spoke, I met a black woman there named Julie Mallory. She and her husband had moved to Las Vegas from the East Coast years ago. He was a railroad ticket agent and had passed away a few years earlier. At one time Las Vegas was a big train stop. I didn't know that any blacks had settled in Las Vegas. I knew there were black students attending Highlands, but that was about it. Mrs. Mallory said, "I've never known a black person to run statewide in New Mexico." She took a handful of my brochures to pass out in her neighborhood.

I campaigned for about a year, about twenty to twenty-five hours a week, before the primary in June 1978. Then, as fate would have it, my good friend Roberto Mondragon won the primary. I finished fourth. That was the last state office I ever ran for. Mondragon teamed up with Bruce King, and they won the election in November.

⁓

The loss surprised me somewhat because I believe I started strong. However, the lack of financial resources eventually became an issue, and I was not able to get my message out to other parts of the state. To tell you the truth, after all that travel, I was kind of glad to take a break. There certainly were exciting times, and I enjoyed getting to meet different people. The long drives were not even too bad; I listened to the radio, mostly country-and-western music, since that was the only musical option. Those drives were conducive to decompressing, reflecting, and planning for things ahead. About 75 percent of my campaigning was done outside Albuquerque. Even though I was physically in good shape, I did get tired from these trips. Quite a few times I would find myself finishing up a rally around midnight and then making the long drive back home to be at work for the Albuquerque Public School District in the morning. I was the school district's equal opportunity director from 1975 to 1987.

At the end of 1978, after having served as a state legislator for ten years, I was ready for a change. I wasn't really certain what that change would be, but I knew it would feel good to have just one job. That's how I felt until I took a walk around my neighborhood park, Hyder Park, where I met an elderly woman sitting on a bench enjoying the scenery. She looked at me, raised her walking cane, and asked, "Young man, don't I know you?" I replied, "Yes ma'am, I live down the street from you." She said, "That's not what I mean. Didn't you used to be somebody?" I answered, "Well, yes, I was somebody at one time, but I guess not anymore." She paused for a moment and then concluded, "That's what I thought."

It was then that I started thinking about running for elected office again. I wanted to still "be somebody." It gets in your blood, you know? In retrospect, I think I laid some of the groundwork for other black men and women in New Mexico to succeed. I didn't really think about it at the time, but, looking back, I believe the fact that I was the first black school principal in Albuquerque and the first black state legislator helped black people in general, especially the younger generation—I believe that my example inspired them. At least, I hope it did. I always tried to carry myself well. I wanted to be a good role model.

As luck would have it, I soon had an offer to run for office again. My good friend Bob Hawk, the county commissioner in my district, called me one day and asked me to have breakfast with him. He told me that he wanted to run for the state legislature and that he would endorse me to run for his commission seat. The office had term limits, and he couldn't run for reelection anymore. So in December 1979 I decided to run.

CHAPTER 12

The Bernalillo County Commission

~~

The idea of serving a larger constituency had been reflected in my decision to run for lieutenant governor, and being a county commissioner would also afford the opportunity to represent a geographically large district. On the surface my direct experience studying and addressing educational and health-related issues did not seem to be relevant; nevertheless, I was comfortable listening to and addressing whatever problems the citizens in my area were facing. During the early 1980s the issues of general concern to Bernalillo County residents centered on economic development, job creation, and property-tax rates.

In December 1979 at the Albuquerque Press Club, I announced my candidacy for District 3 county commissioner. The following was my announcement:

> I wish to take this opportunity to announce my candidacy for Bernalillo county commissioner—District 3. With your help I will be elected and continue to give this district the kind of representation that Mr. Bob Hawk has given for the past six years. I will bring a great deal of experience to the commission, having served ten years as a state representative from District 18—most of that time as chairman of the Education Committee and a member of the Appropriation and Finance Committee. I had an opportunity to know many state, county, and city governments in New Mexico. I will use that experience to bring better representation to the

citizens of this district. I will be one of the individuals speaking for the county before the legislature.

After I made the announcement, I quickly established my campaign team, and everyone was eager to get started. Because of the smaller size of the area that I would serve—a district rather than the entire state—it was easier to organize my campaign team and execute our strategy than it was when I was running for lieutenant governor.

We began raising funds and creating campaign materials such as brochures, yard signs, and bumper stickers. We supplemented our brochures with a letter from County Commissioner Bob Hawk that read as follows:

To The Residents of County Commission District 3: I have served over five years on the Bernalillo County Commission. This year will be my sixth and last year on the commission. I am a candidate for the state legislature. Lenton Malry is a good friend of mine and is a candidate for my position on the County Commission. Lenton is a person who can provide the residents of District 3 with the responsible representation that I believe the people want and deserve. I urge you to support Lenton Malry in his candidacy for County Commissioner representing District 3. Support of Lenton will continue to help make our community the best place to live.

Our door-to-door team consisted of a group of twenty to twenty-five volunteers. These included family members, neighbors, teachers, Kiwanis Club members, church brothers and sisters, Joy's sorority sisters, and coworkers. We would typically meet at my home every Saturday morning at 9:00 a.m. to distribute maps and divide up the assignments of where to go. We would walk around for about four hours, then meet back at my home for a snack and to provide a report on the responses.

I was adamant that we not simply "lit drop"—just leave campaign literature at doors without talking to anyone. I needed feedback, not only about our campaign but also on the issues that resonated with residents. So we took notes and made follow-up telephone calls.

There were about fifty precincts in my district, but I didn't campaign in twelve of them, including the Southeast Heights because that's where I resided. Those twelve precincts encompassed the area I had served as state representative, and people generally already knew me. Our strategy to win this race was to concentrate on the people who didn't know much about me. One challenge of door-to-door campaigning is that you're never sure who's going to vote for you when you give your brochure to people. Most will take your literature with a smile, but that doesn't necessarily correlate with support.

I wanted to put my best foot forward. So, for example, while campaigning I would pick up the newspaper in a front yard and give it to the resident with my brochure inside. I would say, "Here's your paper. I'm Lenton Malry. I would appreciate your vote." I figured they would at least think I was a thoughtful person. I would then spend a couple of minutes with each person discussing issues and what I could do to address them. Some would invite me in for a cup of coffee or a glass of iced tea, but I would respectfully decline because I had many more houses to visit.

Another strategy I employed while campaigning was to invite someone from that neighborhood to walk with me. I thought a familiar face or the fact that the person lived in the area would speak volumes to voters.

Still another strategy I utilized was to visit the county clerk's office and retrieve the names of the residents in all the houses and their party affiliations. We even researched whether someone had voted in the last election. That way, when I went to each door I knew the person's voting history.

A number of houses each had one Democrat and one Republican. So if I talked to Mr. Thompson at the door and he was a Democrat, I would say, "I see you're a Democrat but that your wife is a Republican. Do you think you can convince her to vote for me?" That always got a smile and, I hoped, support.

I enjoyed campaigning and I looked forward to meeting and talking with people. I never considered my race a factor; I just assumed that people would accept me, and I wanted to project that image. I guess I got that optimism from my time in the air force. My former boss, Jack Sheehan, the education officer in London, taught me many things, and he always said, "You're as good as anyone else. I want you to feel that way, and then people will accept you." At that time such a way of thinking was new to me, coming from segregated

Louisiana. When I served in the military I realized that not all blacks were unintelligent and, conversely, that not all whites were intelligent, as I had been led to believe. But because I had been conditioned that way, it took a while for the new awareness to sink in.

As a black child in the deep South, I was conditioned to think that blacks were inferior to whites. It seemed evident from the Jim Crows laws: separate water fountains, bathrooms, cafés, and restaurants. It was a way of life. Once in the early 1980s, when I went back to Shreveport to visit my family, I had to convince my dad that it was okay to sit at the front of the public bus. Old habits—and conditioned ways of thinking—die hard.

But back to the campaign. The general election that fall was fairly easy. I won by a good margin, becoming the first black person to win a county commission seat in New Mexico. Bob Hawk also won election to the legislature, and I thanked him for all his support. Bob resigned his county commission seat early, allowing me to take over in December rather than January, as is customary. It was advantageous to have a head start.

In the beginning of December 1980, Lieutenant Governor Roberto Mondragon came down from Santa Fe to swear me in as county commissioner. Roberto and I had known each other for years, having served in the legislature together. Although he defeated me in the lieutenant governor primary race, I supported him in the general election, and we remained good friends.

To help me transition into my new position, Bob Hawk explained a number of things to me. One situation I wasn't really ready for was long commission meetings every Tuesday night. Some lasted up to four or five hours, depending on the length of the agenda and the number of people who would get up to talk.

A significant portion of the agenda was devoted to zoning issues, and the meetings were often contentious during these discussions. Whenever there was neighborhood opposition to a zoning or development project, it was a recipe for hurt feelings. For example, half the community would support a grocery store with liquor sales or a mobile-home park in their neighborhood, while the other half wouldn't. No matter how you voted, you made half the people angry. And those people were always sitting right in front of you—not like when I was a state representative in Santa Fe and we often voted in a nearly empty chamber.

During my chairmanship of the commission in 1983 and 1984, the job actually affected my sleep. There were several occasions when after a contentious meeting I'd lie awake thinking about some issue we had just tackled. But I was no different from any other elected official who was passionate about the well-being of his or her constituents.

Not all meetings were contentious, though. Many were normal, and some were entertaining because of some of the colorful personalities who testified during public hearings. We had some real characters. I did the best I could to listen to everyone and then make the right decision. It was during this time that I coined my phrase, "Let's roll this train."

Similar to when I served in the legislature, I continued to produce my *Malry-Gram* newsletter to keep the residents in District 3 informed. Here is an excerpt of the *Malry-Gram* in October 1983:

Property Taxes Cut by County

County Commission Chairman Lenton Malry had the pleasure of announcing a tax reduction which goes into effect for property owners in December 1983. Bernalillo County residents and business owners had their property taxes cut by $1.45 per $1,000 of assessed valuation. For example, taxes on a $60,000 house assessed at one-third its market value—$20,000—dropped by $29 a year.

The reduction is due to the refunding of bond issues, early retirement of the Juvenile Detention Center bond issue, revenue-generating investments of bond issue money, and increased collection of delinquent taxes.

"The increased collection of delinquent taxes and the proper funding of investments made it possible to pay off the bonds early and reduce our indebtedness," said Malry.

The tax reduction does not affect the funding of other county projects or services.

I received many letters from the people in District 3 about the property tax; it was a hot topic at that time. Many people believed they were paying too much. I understood their concern but was encouraged that they sought me out as a way to address the issue. I was preparing to run for reelection and, as always, I wanted to be responsive.

Also in that newsletter, I gave a progress report on my first two years on the job:

- Improved rapport with the state legislature
- Planning of the City/County Building
- Closer coordination with the city government
- Sound financial position and balanced budget in Bernalillo County government
- Completion of new addition to the jail and the Bernalillo County Mental Health and Retardation Center

Then I listed my goals:

- Completion of new Burn and Trauma Unit addition in the University of New Mexico Hospital
- One-stop service for payment of city bills and county property taxes in the new City/County Building
- Improved service to Bernalillo County property tax payers through new automated systems in county government
- More efficient data processing and other services for both city and county governments as a result of the new City/County Building

In 1983 there was a major initiative to combine the operations of Bernalillo County and the city of Albuquerque, and this led to the creation of the City/County Building. Many believed that a reduction in the duplication of services would save the taxpayers money. In fact, several pieces of legislation to this effect had failed at the state level. I supported the idea and worked very closely with Mayor Harry Kinney to accomplish it.

We named three city councilors and three county commissioners to collaborate on the project, and I was a member of that team. Voters approved the bond election in 1983 to pay for the City/County Building, but we didn't make much progress in combining city and county operations. This was partly because the commission chairwoman who succeeded me was not in favor of the idea.

I really enjoyed being a commissioner. One of the benefits was that I didn't have to commute between Albuquerque and Santa Fe as I did when I served in the legislature. In addition, county politics were quite interesting and not as intense as serving in the state legislature, which dealt with tighter deadlines and the madness that always occurred at the end of a session. It was a pleasant change.

My term was four years, so in early 1984 I established my reelection committee. It was basically the same team as before. I didn't think I would have any primary opponents, so I was very surprised when I read in the morning newspaper that Alan Reed was going to run against me. Dr. Reed was a professor at the University of New Mexico and one of my good friends. Well, at least I thought he was. Not long before he announced his candidacy, I took him to lunch, and he had told me then that he wasn't going to run for county commissioner. Yet sometime later, without informing me, he changed his mind. I don't know what happened, but needless to say, after that we weren't as close. I decided I would just have to work my tail off in the primary to defeat him.

In March my group of supporters got busy going door-to-door. The two local newspapers endorsed me, and I won the election with almost 58 percent of the vote. On Wednesday, June 6, 1984, the *Albuquerque Tribune* reported as follows:

Perhaps the hardest-fought county primary was for the Democratic nomination in District 3, where incumbent Malry fended off an attack by former City Councilor Reed. . . . Reed said the defeat "wasn't that great a surprise but it was very disappointing. I felt I gave voters good issues and a background in good government. But they decided to go with the other candidate."

Accompanying the article was a picture with the caption "District 3 County Commissioner Lenton Malry flashes a victory sign after winning the Democratic nomination to retain his post."

I felt good enough about my chances of winning in the fall to take the summer off.

On November 6, 1984, I faced Republican Billy Griego. It was the easiest election I had ever run in. I won with more than 60 percent of the vote, and for the first time, instead of having the victory party at my home, my wife and I rented a room at the Sheraton East Hotel to celebrate. We invited a lot of our friends and had a reception. At that time, the Sheraton East (now the Sheraton Albuquerque Uptown, located at Menaul and Louisiana Boulevards) was the place Democrats went to celebrate their victories, and I wanted to be part of that.

The next year my workload increased. Our newly elected governor, Tony Anaya, appointed me to the New Mexico Institute of Mining and Technology (known as New Mexico Tech) board of regents, making it the first time a black person had served on any regents' board in the state. I enjoyed serving in that capacity because it allowed me to reconnect with state educational issues. I was on that board for six years and was the chairman for one year, 1987–1988.

I also took the position of adjunct professor at the University of New Mexico. For fifteen years I taught a course called "Minorities and Politics" on Mondays from 6:15 to 9:15 p.m. The students earned extra credit if they worked on a political campaign. At that time more Hispanics and blacks were becoming involved in politics, and I felt good about encouraging that trend.

In 1984 I also was elected to be a member of the National Association of Counties (NACO) for four years. The organization serves as an advocate on the federal level for all counties in the country. Through education and research it assists in the development of solutions to save counties and taxpayers money. Once again I was the first black member from New Mexico. I had already joined the New Mexico Association of Counties (NMAC) when I was elected county commissioner in 1980, and I was the first black member of that organization as well. In 1985 I was elected first vice president of NMAC. I was the only one in the history of the organization to serve as an official for more than one year. The Lord has truly blessed me.

In the summer of 1985 NMAC was conducting a legislative meeting in Albuquerque. In previous years I had attended the meetings only occasionally, but since this one was in Albuquerque I had no hesitation in attending it. They happened to be holding elections for the next year's offices, and they had an opening for first vice president because the current man in the office was leaving to become a cabinet secretary for Governor Garrey Caruthers. That meant the association had to find a replacement to fill his remaining six months.

A county commissioner from Los Alamos nominated me, and I got elected! To hold office in NMAC today, you usually have to start as second vice president and work your way up. Then in January 1986 I was elected president of NMAC, with no one even running against me.

It was great to work with Donna Smith, the executive director of NMAC. She had been a lobbyist in Santa Fe when I was a state representative. I had the opportunity to travel around the state and meet with all the other county commissioners. I also made appointments to committees and presided over our two annual meetings. Our legislative meetings were always held in January in Santa Fe, and our summer meetings were held in different cities around the state. I made many friends around the state and was also invited to speak in a number of towns when I was president.

Then I was elected to NACO and served with that group from 1984 until 1988.

I served as chairman of the Bernalillo County Commission from 1983 to 1984 and was reelected for 1987 to 1988. Those were my last two years on the commission, and I also retired from the Albuquerque Public School District in 1987. I was beginning to think about setting up a private affirmative-action consulting firm.

In the summer of 1988, knowing that my county commissioner term would end in December, I began to think about what other constituents I could serve and in what capacity. My current congressman, Manuel Lujan, announced that he would not run for reelection. Several friends suggested I give it a shot. At that time the congressional district included Bernalillo, Torrance, and Guadalupe Counties.

I again established my campaign team and began raising funds. I mostly campaigned in Albuquerque, but I also attended many events in Moriarty and Santa Rosa. A major challenge for me was raising enough funds to compete successfully. I raised about $60,000 from donors that included the Black Congressional Caucus and Mervyn Dymally from California. Unfortunately, I needed almost twice that amount to compete with the other candidates. Given that reality, I was ultimately unsuccessful in my attempt and lost the election. That was my last race for elected office.

My good friend Tom Udall won the Democratic nomination, and I was happy to support him in the general election. He unfortunately lost the election to Steve Schiff. That congressional district was Republican and stayed that way for the next twenty years. In 2008, however, the district turned Democratic with the election of Martin Heinrich. He was a neighbor of mine, and I was pleased to help him on his campaign. I had also worked on his first run for office, which was for city councilor. For the congressional race he ran a great campaign. For instance, he strategically opened a campaign office in the South Valley in an effort to garner support and interest in that area, and he had his staff members attend all neighborhood-association meetings in the district and provide impressive, informative presentations. I hosted a campaign fund-raiser for him and was elated to see him win. He served the district very well and went on to run successfully for the US Senate, where he has held his seat since 2012.

Our current congressional representative is Michelle Lujan-Grisham, whom I also eagerly supported. She continues to represent the district very well.

CHAPTER 13

Malry and Associates, 1987–1992

A fter retiring from the school district in June 1987, I got pretty restless. Although I still served as county commissioner and taught at the university, I was curious about starting a business.

One of my best friends, an attorney named Larry Lamb, suggested that I should start my own affirmative-action consulting firm. Its purpose would be to help local businesses and governments understand the affirmative-action laws.

I remember when President John F. Kennedy signed Executive Order 10925, on March 6, 1961, which established the Equal Employment Opportunity Commission (EEOC). The order stated that contractors doing business with the government "will take affirmative action to ensure that applicants are employed, and employees are treated during their employment, without regard to their race, creed, color, or national origin." The order did not advocate preferential treatment of affected groups but rather sought to eliminate discrimination in the traditional sense. The legal status of affirmative action was solidified by the Civil Rights Act of 1964.

Larry drew up the paperwork, and we created a corporation, Malry and Associates. I was the president, Lenny was the vice president, and Joy (who was already working elsewhere) was the secretary-treasurer. After filing a business application with the New Mexico Corporation Commission in Santa Fe and securing liability insurance, I was in business. Well, let's put it this way: I was *ready* to do business. All I needed were some clients.

My first client was First National Bank in Albuquerque. The bank's officials wanted me to train their managers on how to avoid affirmative-action lawsuits. They had had some grievances filed against them, and I was going to be their first professional advisor.

One of the first things I did was hire a local attorney named Marsha Hardeman to work part-time for my company. I had known Marsha for years and thought highly of her legal skills. She had previously worked as an attorney and as the human-resources director for the city of Albuquerque. Marsha conducted affirmative-action workshops for our clients. She knew that subject up one side and down the other, and she was also a good speaker. We held one or two workshops a month, each one lasting around three hours. In addition, Marsha helped me teach my political-science class at the university.

The next contract I got was with the local utility company, PNM (Public Service Company of New Mexico). It wanted me to conduct meetings all over town with people who were having trouble paying their PNM bills. Although this was not directly related to affirmative-action guidance, it did provide a community service. I held three or four meetings a month. They were always free and were held in the early evening, typically in the South Valley, to accommodate people who worked during the day. Fifteen to twenty people usually came to each meeting.

I remember one man who had lost his job and didn't have heat in his apartment because he didn't have enough money to pay his PNM bill. He had a wife and two children, and this family was trying to get through the winter in a freezing apartment. I put him in touch with the PNM department that handled such cases. The company turned the heat on again, and he eventually found another job. Once more it felt good to be able to help someone.

Later I received a contract with Bill Johnson, the chief executive officer of the University of New Mexico hospital. I arranged for him to speak at local service-club meetings, like the Kiwanis Club and the Rotary Club. He would explain that the hospital was of benefit to the city, county, and state, not just to the university. Our company set up about two speaking engagements a month for Bill during the year and a half that we had that contract. At that time the hospital was named the Bernalillo County Medical Center, and its image was not particularly good. It predominantly served uninsured people who needed medical help. It was in transition and wanted to improve its image. I think we helped it do so.

Then I received my biggest contract ever. The city of Albuquerque paid us $10,000 a month to handle all its affirmative-action grievances. I had to hire staff and set up offices in the Western Bank Building downtown. The city of Albuquerque was my favorite client as well as my largest client, and it didn't require any out-of-town travel.

This was the first time I had ever worked for myself, and I enjoyed having my own company. I had a great staff, and business was going well. Our caseload varied from month to month, but we always had enough work to keep us busy. I also joined the Albuquerque Chamber of Commerce and the Economic Forum so I could increase my network and obtain more clients.

My next contract was with Sunwest Bank, which hired me to promote its new project, the Advantage Program for Seniors. The bank's goal was to cultivate more business with senior citizens. I distributed information on services such as free checking and specialized consulting, and I connected with retired-teachers associations and senior-affairs groups. That contract lasted nearly two years and had me traveling around the state—wherever there was a Sunwest Bank—on four or five out-of-town speaking engagements a month, talking to groups about the advantages of signing up for the program. I would go to places like Farmington, Gallup, Santa Fe, Raton, Silver City, Clovis, Las Cruces, Roswell, and Hobbs.

On a typical day, for instance, I might drive to Farmington, 180 miles away, to meet with representatives from the teacher's association and then with the local bank representative to assess and plan our next meeting; then on the same afternoon I would drive to Gallup, another 110 miles, and meet with the bank representative that evening. The next day I would meet with teachers in Gallup and then head back to Albuquerque, 140 miles away, by the evening. It reminded me of my travels campaigning for lieutenant governor!

The bank owned a plane, and at times I was able to coordinate a flight with other bank officials traveling to the same destination. Most of the time, however, I drove myself. Except for all those hours behind the wheel, I really enjoyed the trips, meeting different people from all around the state, some of whom I already knew from my time in the state legislature.

Usually I was well received everywhere I went, but I do remember a weird incident that happened in Hobbs. (It seemed like every time I went to address a crowd in Hobbs, something bad would happen!) I went there to give a speech to promote Sunwest Bank's Advantage Program for Seniors, and I was greeting people at the door before they took their seats. A couple came in and didn't say a word to me, and when I stood up to give my talk, they walked out. They either didn't like me or didn't like Sunwest Bank, but I assumed it was because I'm black. No one ever said anything, and I never actually found out why they left, but of course I didn't feel good about it. I just considered it to be their loss, and I didn't let it linger in my mind. I had flown down on the company plane, so I was able to leave right away. I didn't stick around.

In the spring of 1990 the economy took a downturn, and many of the contracts I had were not renewed. The first to go was PNM, where I was working for David Rusk, a longtime Southeast Heights friend. We had worked together in politics for many years. He and I had served in the state legislature together, and I had also helped him to get elected mayor of Albuquerque. When he wasn't reelected, he took a job with PNM. Then he called me in one day and told me that the company was not renewing my contract. It wasn't a matter of performance, it was simply based on the economy.

The next client to go was Sunwest Bank. The special program that I was promoting for it had ended after only one year.

My biggest loss was the city of Albuquerque. After Louis Saavedra was elected mayor, the city told me that its affirmative-action cases would be handled in-house, so it would no longer need my services. Eventually all that was left was our contract with UNM Hospital (the former Bernalillo County Medical Center), and I had to let my staff go—three full-time employees. I called everybody in to a meeting to notify them. I said I was sorry, and it was a very painful meeting. My first private-sector job was failing.

Shortly after that, Bill Johnson of UNM Hospital contacted me and indicated that he had a full-time job open. So in the summer of 1990 I began working in the personnel department at the hospital, providing training and doing some interviewing. I kept my consulting firm, though, hoping that one day I might be able to make a comeback. I moved into a smaller office and kept renewing my license for the next few months, but we never got it up and running again.

To stay connected to politics, I volunteered to work on Bruce King's gubernatorial campaign. He had been governor twice before and had served the state well. Thus, in the spring of 1990 I handed out literature door-to-door, made phone calls, hosted fund-raisers, and organized and attended many rallies. King won the election in November 1990, and my good friend James Lewis was named the governor's chief of staff. There was a possibility that I too might be fortunate enough to work in Governor King's administration.

CHAPTER 14

State Government

In January 1991 things were going pretty well for me and my family. Joy was teaching at Kirtland Elementary School, and although Lenny had lost his job as an Albuquerque city planner because of budget cuts, he was able to quickly get another job, with the Dona Ana County Planning Department in Las Cruces.

The night before the swearing in of Governor Bruce King, Joy and I went to Santa Fe for the big celebration with my attorney friend Larry Lamb and his wife, Kay. My good friend James Lewis had asked me to meet him around 9:00 p.m. at the Hilton Hotel, and I was hoping that he would tell me that the governor had a job for me. It seemed that 9:00 p.m. would never come, but when it finally did, James informed me that I was going to be the state's human-rights director. The Human Rights Division, which had a staff of about twenty, was responsible for handling all state employee grievances based on age, sex, and race. I really wanted a position in Albuquerque rather than having to drive sixty-five miles to Santa Fe every weekday, but I was happy about the appointment. James told me to go to the Human Rights office and tell the current director that I was replacing him. I did, and he just packed his things and left. He knew how politics worked in Santa Fe.

The next week the following item appeared in the *Albuquerque Tribune*:

Former Bernalillo County Commissioner Lenton Malry has landed a $47,000 a year job as the director of the Human Rights Division of the

State's Department of Labor. Malry, who retired from the Albuquerque Public Schools, said he'll continue to draw his APS retirement checks as well as his new salary. The former county commissioner was named to the post on Jan. 2 by Gov. Bruce King.

Although this was a political appointment, my twelve years of experience as the director of the EEOC for APS made me more than qualified and a natural fit.

Later I found out that there were some people in the governor's administration and my office who weren't very happy that I was "double-dipping"—drawing a retirement check from APS while still earning a good salary from the state. No one said anything directly to me about it, but I heard rumors. I just ignored them and did my job.

While the state legislature was in session, I would visit it and discuss my department budget as well as any legislation that affected the department and its constituents. Many of the same legislators I had worked with in the 1970s were still there, and they were very good to me. I also had a great staff at the Human Rights Division. Most of the staff members had worked there for many years, so they knew their jobs and did them well.

During my first year on the job, I found out that there was a vacancy on the state Human Rights Board. I called the governor's office, which told me to compile a list of candidates for the position. After looking at the applications and having my staff review them, I called and made an appointment with the governor to discuss the vacancy. In that meeting I got a real education. Governor King called in some of his staff and told them, "First, I want you to see how much money each of those individuals gave my election campaign. Second, I want to know how well I ran in his or her county." After they gave him that information, he told me who would get the appointment. On the way back to my office, I said to myself, "That's the way they do things up here!"

The following week I went to Washington, DC, to attend a conference. When I checked into the hotel, the woman at the desk looked at me funny and said, "Call the governor of New Mexico right away." I quickly went to my room and called Governor King. He said, "When you get back Monday, come and see me." When I went to his office, he said he had heard that I now had a vacancy in my office. I said, "Yes, I do," and he told me to interview a young man from Las Vegas, New Mexico. I told him I would, and at the end of the week I gave that man a job. I clearly remembered how that appointment was filled.

Later I asked Governor King if I could get enough money to put a Human Rights Division branch office in Albuquerque. I told him it was hard for some state employees who didn't live in Santa Fe to make the trip there to file grievances. He told me to talk to a few legislators about the matter, which I did, but we couldn't get all the money we needed in the first year. However, we did put two members of our staff in Albuquerque at the state Labor Department building on Broadway. I really wanted them to have their own office, but the governor said, "Wait one year, and they will have funding for their own place."

The governor then asked where I wanted the office to be, and I told him I wanted space in the Western Bank Building downtown because that's where the EEOC was located. Sometimes an individual would not know whether to file a grievance with us, the state, or the federal government. Having our office there would make it easier for people to file their grievances regardless of whom it was with. The next year we got our wish, and that was one of the best things I accomplished while running the department. Currently, the Human Rights office is still located at the Western Bank Building, and some of the employees have thanked me for saving them from having to commute to Santa Fe. But more important, it has made it more convenient for our Albuquerque citizens to access the service.

On a more personal note, in January 1991 I was also dealing with the loss of my mother, who passed away suddenly of a heart attack. One night she called my brother Clinton and asked him to bring her some Pepto-Bismol because she said she had indigestion. When he got to her house and saw what she looked like, he called an ambulance. She died on the way to the hospital, and Dad and Clinton were with her.

To say Dad was brokenhearted would be an understatement. He was just lost. He and Mom had been married for sixty-nine years. He didn't want to live with any of his sons after Mom died; he wanted to stay in his own home. A month or so later, doctors had to amputate one of his legs because he got gangrene. Apparently he had cut his foot with a hoe in his garden one day and didn't go to the doctor until it was too late. I went to see him in the hospital, and he had a strange look on his face. He never got over losing his leg; he couldn't adjust. He kept saying, "Look, my leg is gone," and then he would cry. I told him that things were going to be okay and that he was going to get an artificial leg. We had to put him in a nursing home in Shreveport. I flew down there once, and when I asked the director how Dad was doing, she said he was having a hard time. She was sympathetic toward him and was doing the best she could for him. Dad wanted to go home, but he couldn't live there alone anymore. Three weeks after he moved into the nursing home, he passed away.

I then made a point of visiting my older brother, John, in Los Angeles. We called our brother Clinton in Shreveport and discussed what to do with our parents' home and rental properties.

While this was occurring, I was also having a challenging time at work. Two employees falsely charged me with sexual harassment in what was actually a case of employee retaliation. It all began with my chief administrative officer leaving the division for a job promotion in the private sector. I wanted to fill the vacancy with a highly qualified candidate regardless of whether the person had worked in state government before. One candidate from outside state government was interested in the position, but we were not able to meet his desired salary. Therefore I focused on two candidates from within the division, both of whom were women. One lived in Albuquerque, and I had assigned her to the newly opened Albuquerque office so she did not have to commute to Santa Fe every day. The other candidate was from Santa Fe.

I selected the employee from Santa Fe for the position. This created an instant division among the employees, including my administrative assistant, who had lobbied aggressively for the other employee, her close friend. In addition, the selected employee was not very well liked by several staff members, but I believed her to be a good worker and the better choice. This was mistake number one.

Another employee, also closely aligned with the person not selected, was on probation and was proving to be a problem employee. He would arrive to work late and socialize too much, and he didn't treat the newly selected individual, who was his new supervisor, with respect. This was widely known. With my concurrence, his new supervisor provided him with a memo outlining job expectations and corrective measures. He became verbally combative and even balled up the memo and threw it in her face! This was totally unacceptable, so I immediately contacted Human Resources and asked for guidance. I was told that since he was probationary, he could be terminated, so I fired him. Now I became disliked by half the division—mistake number two.

One of the staffers informed me that several people in the office were attempting to have me removed. She indicated that she would not attend the meeting or take part in the group's efforts.

About a week later, while I was meeting with the governor on some legislative issues, he informed me that one of my staffers, the one from Albuquerque whom I hadn't selected, had informed him that she was charging me with sexual harassment. I explained that I was innocent of any inappropriate behavior and told him about the events that had transpired within the division. He indicated that I should have informed him before I fired the problem employee. This was mistake number three.

To my surprise, my administrative assistant filed a sexual harassment charge the next week. It was apparent that the group's tactics were working. As if all this weren't enough, the former employee I had terminated made several threats. This concerned me enough to notify my family.

I was placed on administrative leave. This was becoming an increasingly negative issue for the governor, who was running for reelection. There was no doubt in my mind that it was more than mere coincidence that this was occurring just several months after black Supreme Court nominee Clarence Thomas had been accused of sexual harassment by Anita Hill, and it had captivated the nation through the nominating process and testimony shown on television. Governor King did not want this issue to escalate. He called me to his office and presented me with the option of either resigning or being terminated. Advised by my lawyer, I chose not to resign, since I was innocent and wanted to defend myself at a hearing. I was then terminated.

After several months of investigation and just before the governor left office, the case was settled by the state. This disappointed me greatly, since I was not able to have my day in court.

In the summer of 1992 I concentrated on taking care of settling my parents' estate in Shreveport, which was very time-consuming. My mother and father had owned several rental properties, and Clinton and I were trying to sell all the houses. I made several trips back and forth between Albuquerque and Shreveport. About a year later we had sold all the houses, including Mom and Dad's home. By then Lenny had left Las Cruces and had taken a planning job with the city of Rio Rancho, which was experiencing significant population growth. I wanted to return to working in education.

However, there was a problem with that idea. If you retired in the education field in New Mexico, you could make only a certain amount of money if you came back—I believe it was $14,000 a year. So instead I applied for a few positions in California, but nothing panned out. In February 1993 I applied for a personnel director job with the Window Rock Unified School System, headquartered in Fort Defiance, Arizona.

CHAPTER 15

My Return to the Navajo Reservation

⁓ℳ⁓

The opportunity to work in Arizona allowed me to receive my full retirement income in New Mexico. That was my whole motivation for applying for the position of personnel director at the Window Rock Unified School System. I forwarded a few letters of recommendations, one of which was from a former coworker at Albuquerque Public Schools, Patrick Kelly, who wrote the following:

> As you engage in the process of screening applicants for the position
> of Personnel Director, I would like to bring to your attention the name
> of an outstanding applicant—Dr. Lenton Malry. I had the pleasure of
> working with Dr. Malry for ten years at the Albuquerque Public Schools.
> At the time, he was the Director of the Equal Employment Opportunity
> office and I was his Assistant. I came to know Dr. Malry very well during
> that span of time, and feel that I can speak with conviction about his
> qualifications.

In March 1993 I was called in for an interview. I appeared before a committee of about ten people from the Window Rock school system. I shared with them my experience teaching at the Navajo reservation's Kinlichee School, which was about thirty miles away, and I told them that I had served in the New Mexico legislature with Leo Watchman, a state representative from that area on the New Mexico side (Window Rock Unified Schools is on the

Arizona–New Mexico border). Although legally his constituents were in New Mexico only, the committee appeared interested.

A few days later Superintendent Floyd Ashley called to inform me that I had been recommended by the committee. He was going to be in Albuquerque the next day and wanted to interview me, so I invited him to come by my home. We talked for about an hour. He inquired about my background, and I mentioned my experience working on the reservations with both the Navajo and Zuni tribes. He asked me to attend the school-board meeting on the next Tuesday and requested that I arrive early to meet with him first.

I did just that, but when I met with him he told me that the Window Rock School Board might not approve my application because the board members wanted him to select Navajos for all administrative positions. He said he would do his best to get me approved. I knew one board member's father, Sam Billerson, from when I worked in Kinlichee, but I didn't know if that would help me. Sam's son greeted me when he came in with the other four school-board members, and then they went into another room to meet privately in a special session for several hours. I didn't think they were ever going to come out.

I didn't know any of the school board's staff, but the high school principal was very friendly. He kept talking to me and let me call Joy around 10:00 p.m. so I could tell her that I was going to be late getting home.

About 10:15 p.m. the entire school board came out and asked me to come up to the front of the room because they wanted to ask me a few questions. They asked me mostly about my family: "Are you married? Any children?" I don't know why they asked those things, but I assume they wanted a family man. They also asked me how soon I could start, and I told them next Monday. They concluded that they were going to follow Superintendent Ashley's recommendation and offer me the job, but they didn't look very happy about it. Later I found out that it was not personal, they just rarely expressed any feelings in that setting. The board welcomed me to the team, and I looked forward to the job. I was extremely happy and grateful, and I immediately notified Joy. Because of the distance—I would live in Fort Defiance during the week and come home to Albuquerque only on weekends—she wasn't thrilled, but she knew that I wouldn't be happy sitting idly in Albuquerque. So it was for the best.

I began working for Window Rock Unified Schools in March and made the drive home every weekend. It took two and half to three hours each way. Lenny had gotten a job with the city of Rio Rancho, so he was able to stay with Joy when I was gone during the week.

On my first day, around 7:30 a.m., I reported to Superintendent Ashley's office. He told me about the school district and what was expected from me and my office. He then took me around to meet the staff—two women and one man, all Navajos. I could tell we were all going to get along just fine. They were used to working with non-Natives; my predecessor was white.

Work hours were 8:00 a.m. to 5:00 p.m. I always got to the office around 7:30 a.m. and didn't leave until 5:30 p.m. or later. My dad had told me years ago to always get to the office earlier than your staff and stay later. I had no problem with that idea, since I lived alone. I had nothing to do after work but eat dinner and watch television. I had brought a TV set with me from Albuquerque, and I gained some weight from eating a lot of frozen dinners. When I got home each evening, I would called Joy in Albuquerque, watch the news on television, read, and then go to sleep.

As personnel director, I was in charge of all interviewing and hiring. My staff and I also handed out paychecks. I had a hardworking staff, and to reward my employees I took them to lunch every two weeks. My salary was about $50,000, similar to what I had earned in New Mexico. I was really excited to be back in education; it was where I wanted to be, where I was most comfortable. I really enjoyed my job and my work with the community.

After I had been on the job for a week, Superintendent Ashley came over to my office and told me that he liked my work ethic. "You put in a lot of extra hours, so you can take off early on Fridays," he said. On some Fridays, however, I would stay after work and watch the high school football games before heading to Albuquerque. I wanted to be part of the school community, and I became close friends with the high school principal.

In April Joy informed me that she was going to retire at the end of the school year, and she would come and live with me in Fort Defiance. Although most of the school employees lived in Fort Defiance, where the school-district offices were located, the district offered Joy and me a nice three-bedroom home it had bought in Window Rock, about five miles east of Fort Defiance.

In May Superintendent Ashley gave me an extra assignment. The school board had voted to give teachers extra money for any college credits they earned after getting their degrees. My new assignment involved verifying their transcripts. This involved contacting the colleges and universities to get updated transcripts. It took me a few weeks to complete the assignment.

I could tell that Superintendent Ashley appreciated me. He included me in all the big decisions that were made. Once, when there was a bill before the Arizona legislature that would give our school district the funds to expand, he told me that he wanted me to travel with him to Phoenix to lobby for the bill. We left early one morning and met with the senator of our district, who said he would do what he could. We were ultimately successful in receiving additional funding for the following school year.

I was very happy when Joy was finished with school and was finally able to live with me in Window Rock. I was glad to have my companion back. We went to the movies, went shopping, and bought food for the home-cooked meals I was so fond of. I had certainly grown tired of those frozen dinners! I also enjoyed barbecuing on the back patio. The house we were given to live in was in a very nice area, and I was very happy with it. It had all the modern conveniences that my home in Albuquerque had. There was a big difference between our life in Fort Defiance in 1959 and our experience in 1993.

Those were special days. I told Superintendent Ashley that Joy would like a teaching job with the school district. Shortly after that she had an interview and was hired as a first-grade teacher. Now we were both retired from jobs in New Mexico and working in Arizona. Lenny was taking care of the house in Albuquerque, and his job in the city of Rio Rancho was going well.

Even though Joy was now living with me in Window Rock, we would still go back to Albuquerque every weekend. It was home, and we wanted to connect with our relatives and friends, whom we missed seeing, and attend our church on Sunday. Then on Sunday afternoon we would return to Window Rock.

Although I enjoyed my job with Superintendent Ashley and the school district, I ended up working in Arizona for less than a year. In late October Joy and I found out that her youngest sister, Sherry, had breast cancer. She and Joy's other two sisters lived in Albuquerque, so Joy and I talked about the situation and decided to move back to help the family through a tough time. We didn't know how serious it was, but we wanted to be there for them. In addition, I missed home more than I thought I would, and I had begun to consider finding a job in Albuquerque.

The next weekend I was home, I went to lunch with my attorney and friend Larry Lamb and told him about my situation. He told me that Motorola was hiring some trainers to make operations better and faster. I put in my application, took a day off from work, and went for an interview. Two days before Thanksgiving in 1993 I received a call offering me a position. I had prayed in earnest, and I thanked the Lord.

Joy and I always hosted Thanksgiving dinner for our relatives and friends, and that year at Thanksgiving dinner we made the announcement that we were moving back home. It was a happy occasion.

My excitement was tempered, however, when I informed Superintendent Ashley. He was sad because we had formed a great team and had become very close. His wife told me that the day I told him that I was leaving, he didn't sleep all night. I had enjoyed working with him the previous eight months.

The school district had a big going-away party for Joy and me and gave us many gifts, including handmade Navajo rugs. One of my favorites was a wall clock with WINDOW ROCK inscribed on it.

We left Window Rock a few days before the Christmas break. Joy's sister Eleanor and her husband, Jim Jones, came up to Window Rock the day that I was leaving. While Joy and I were at work they cleaned the house and packed the U-Haul trailer. They did a great job, and I still feel indebted to them for all they did. When Joy and I got off work, we drove to Albuquerque. It sure felt good to be home, and I took Joy and Lenny out to dinner to celebrate. The next day I started working at Motorola.

Presentation at the Albuquerque Public School Board, Albuquerque, New Mexico, 1980 (courtesty of the *Albuquerque Tribune*)

Swearing in as Bernalillo county commissioner, 1980

With Senator Edward Kennedy and his wife, Joan, 1980

With NBC *Today*'s Willard Scott, 1980

With Betty Brown and Senator Jeff Bingaman at a conference in Albuquerque, 1982

VOLUME III   A MALRY NEWSLETTER   OCTOBER 1983

LENTON MALRY HIS RECORD

For those new residents of District 3 this Malry-gram includes a brief explanation of the record of County Commission Chairman Lenton Malry.

Lenton Malry's dedication to public service continues with his work in the county commission. His years as State Representative of District 18 gave him the experience and knowledge necessary to ably fulfill his present role as county commission chairman.

At the State House of Representatives Malry was at the forefront in the areas of education, health care and senior citizens' concerns.

Malry served as chairman of the Education Committee, Chairman of the Health and Aging Committee and as a member of the Appropriations and Finance Committee.

During his years as a state representative, he was lauded for sponsoring the Kindergarten bill and for assuring passage of legislation providing better funding for public schools and higher education.

Malry has also been very active in community affairs. He served as a member of the Board of Directors for: National Council of Christians and Jews, NAACP, Alum Association of UNM, State Vocational Council, Sickle Cell Council, Hearing and Speech Center, St. Anthony Boys Home, Metropolitan Criminal Justice Council.

In 1972 Malry was appointed to WICHE (Western Interstate Commission for Higher Education) where he served as chairman in 1975-76.

PROPERTY TAXES CUT BY COUNTY

County Commission Chairman Lenton Malry had the pleasure of announcing a tax reduction which goes into effect for property owners in December, 1983.

Bernalillo County Residents and business owners had their property taxes cut by $1.45 per $1,000 of assessed valuation. For example, taxes on a $60,000 house assessed at one-third its market value — $20,000 — dropped by $29 a year.

The reduction is due to the refunding of bond issues, early retirement of the Juvenile Detention Center bond issue, revenue-generating investments of bond issue money and increased collection of delinquent taxes.

"The increased collection of delinquent taxes and the proper funding of investments made it possible to pay off the bonds early and reduce our indebtedness," said Malry.

The tax reduction does not affect the funding of other county projects or services.

Citizen reaction to the reduction is reflected in the letter printed below which a county resident penned to a newspaper . . .

HAPPY WITH REDUCTION

I THINK that we should indeed be proud of Bernalillo County Commission Chairman Lenton Malry, and the other commissioners as well, for reducing property taxes.

I have lived in this county my entire life, and I cannot recall when the city or the county reduced our taxes. There is usually a way found to spend any type of surplus.

I also heard Chairman Malry state on television news that he personally would like to do away with property taxes, and finance local government on income and sales taxes. I happen to agree with this particular philosophy.

I am very pleased the commissioners are thinking about their constituency — keep up the good work!

    TOM COOPER
    Albuquerque

The *Malry-Gram*, 1983

Speaking at the dedication of the University of New Mexico Hospital Burn Unit, which I helped pass legislation for as a commissioner, 1984

With Governors Gary Carruthers of New Mexico (left), Edwin Edwards of Louisiana, and Dona Smith of New Mexico, Association of Counties, 1987

New Mexico Institute of Mining and Technology board of regents, 1987

With Lenton Jr. and Joy, 1990

With my brothers, John (left) and Clinton (right), 1991

With my good friend James Lewis, the chief of staff to Governor Bruce King, 1991 (courtesy of *Round the Roundhouse*)

With Alex Abeyta, the Bernalillo County treasurer

With (left to right) Joy; Joy's sister, Eleanor Jones; Eleanor's husband, Jim Jones; and Joy's eldest sister, Dorothy Cook

Joy and me, 1995

Working at Corley's Car
Dealership, 1997

Keynote speaker at the
Joint Session of the Leg-
islature, First African
American Day, 1999
(courtesy of the *Santa Fe
New Mexican*)

Induction to Grambling
State University Hall of
Fame, 2007

Our fiftieth wedding anniversary, 2008

With my church family, led by Pastor Michael Cook (far right), 2009

With my childhood best friend, Booker T. Bennett

With my first cousin, Janie Mae Jack

Joy and me, 2012

Our political weekly Saturday morning breakfast

COUSIN LENTON
Lenton Malry

Which reminds me, I am having lunch today with my "cousin," Dr. Lenton Malry who was the first black elected to the Legislature from NM. Democrat Lenton, a former Bernalillo county commissioner who now works as the county's neighborhood program coordinator, has served as an analyst for every one of my Election Night broadcasts on KANW 89.1 FM since way back in 88.' Today I will tell him to not spoil the October 4 Election Night by predicting the winners too early.

Get out the credit card, Lenton. Once a politico, always one, which gives you the honor.

Thanks for joining me today. Hope to see you again tomorrow.

(c)NM POLITICS WITH JOE MONAHAN 2005
Not for reproduction without permission of the author

Posted by: Joe Monahan / 9/13/2005 12:01:00 AM

Joe Monahan's blog, September 13, 2005 (courtesy of *New Mexico Politics with Joe Monahan*)

My second retirement from Bernalillo County, 2011

CHAPTER 16

Motorola

My job as a trainer at Motorola was the first time that I had worked for a private company other than my own consulting firm, Malry and Associates. To say that working for a large multinational corporation was different from working in the public sector is an understatement. Working for a telecommunications company was exciting, however, because I was fascinated by new technology (I suppose that fascination began on the farm in Louisiana when my Dad purchased the big new Firestone radio that was our major entertainment source). The focus of Motorola was on making a profit and ensuring that all the processes were efficient and effective. In fact, in the mid-1980s Motorola had invented the Six Sigma quality-improvement process, which became the global standard.

I enjoyed the change in focus from my previous jobs. The training sessions I conducted consisted of several hour-long sessions every day in which the employees learned how to produce a better product faster. The most challenging class began at 7:00 a.m., for the workers getting off the overnight shift. I imagine the last thing they wanted to do at that time was attend a training session! Some of these workers would fall asleep during class, and I would have to ask one of the guys next to them to wake them up. There was one guy in that class who didn't pay attention at all but simply spent the entire time chitchatting with some of the other men at the back of the room. I constantly had to ask him to pay attention—he was always talking when he should have been listening. He actually reminded me of myself when I got in trouble for talking in class and was disciplined by both my teacher and later at home by Dad. I tried to be relatively gentle, but I had to remind him often, because his talking was distracting to the other students.

I can't remember anyone saying anything inappropriate to me except once, when a guy came to class one morning, saw me, and said, "You're black, aren't you?" And I replied, "All day I'll be black." He looked at me in a funny way. I picked up that line while I was stationed in England in the air force and would occasionally run into airmen from the United States.

I earned a good salary at Motorola and knew the general manager from my legislative days, which was also helpful. My office was just down the hall from his, and he would stop by and talk to me from time to time. He would ask, "How are you enjoying it here? What do you think of the students? Can I do anything to make things better for you?" After I had been there three months or so, he sent me to Phoenix for a four-day training session. I was able to take Joy, now that she had retired. While I was in class, she would go shopping. In the evening we would attend a movie or go out for dinner. Some nights we would do both. This was the spring of 1994, and some evenings we would sit in a park near the hotel. I enjoyed having Joy with me, and the workshops were fun and educational.

Once I had settled into the job, my supervisor gave me additional duties. For example, I would talk to faculty members in the UNM Engineering Department to determine how many students were about to graduate. Then I would recruit some of those students to work for Motorola. In addition, I performed some community-outreach activities, such as being part of a team that handed out Thanksgiving turkeys to needy families.

Another aspect of my job that I enjoyed was checking out the assembly lines. For maybe an hour a day I would go downstairs and watch the line moving, so I could determine whether there was any way to improve our processes.

I really enjoyed working at Motorola. Management took good care of me and was generous to the workers in general. For example, at Christmas the employees received bonus checks, which management called "sharing in the profit" and issued to show its gratitude. I was pleasantly surprised to receive a bonus check the first year, since I had worked for the company for only a few months.

During that time Joy's sister Sherry was being treated for cancer, and it was beginning to take its toll on her. On some weekends we would spend time with her and her two daughters. Sherry, like the rest of us, had gone into education, and during the last year of her life she taught school. To keep her medical insurance, Joy and her sister Eleanor would substitute-teach for Sherry when she was too ill. Eleanor, like Joy, had retired, so they worked for free to enable their sister to keep her job and her insurance. Sherry had graduated from the Texas University Women's College in Denton, Texas. Some friends she made there encouraged her to join them in Lubbock, Texas. She did, and she held a teaching position there for several years. Sherry never married, but she adopted two girls while she was teaching in Lubbock. Later she followed Joy and Eleanor to Albuquerque and taught at Alamosa Elementary School for several years.

I worked at Motorola for more than a year. In the summer of 1995 Eddie Corley Sr., from Grants, New Mexico, called me and said he had just bought the Lincoln-Mercury dealership in Albuquerque, and could we meet for lunch?

I had known Eddie for years, ever since he owned a couple of gas stations in Grants. I had driven through Grants a few times and was surprised to see a black man in that town. He told me he came from Texas. He was very open and very friendly. I knew that he owned the Ford dealership in Grants, but I did not realize that he also owned the Plymouth dealership in Gallup. When he told me that he was moving to Albuquerque and wanted to talk to me, I had a sense that he needed something, but I didn't know what. So I invited him and his son, Eddie Jr., to go to a Kiwanis Club meeting with me. We had a good visit, and he told me, "You know everyone in this town. I want you to come and work for me." I agreed initially to work part-time, four days a week.

I gave my notice to Motorola in the fall of 1995. Management was a little disappointed, but I explained that I was going to help a friend who was beginning a new business venture.

CHAPTER 17

The Albuquerque
Lincoln-Mercury Dealership

$\mathcal{M}$

From 1995 to 2000 I held two jobs at
the Lincoln-Mercury dealership. One
was public-relations director, and the other was to monitor and decide which
salesmen would use the phone room each day. The phone room contained
a bank of phones for the sales staff to use to solicit business. Eddie Sr. was
present at the Albuquerque site during the week but would go back to his
home in Grants for the weekend. Eddie Jr. was present at the Albuquerque
site most of the time.

When Eddie Sr. couldn't appear at a social event, I would represent the
dealership for him. I spoke to local service clubs like the Rotary and Kiwanis
Clubs and shared with them information about the Corley family and the
dealership. In addition, I took advantage of every opportunity to market the
dealership. I would say, "We would surely like to have your business." It was
an unadulterated sales pitch, and I was always happy to give it. I was very
happy working at the dealership. I got to see many old friends who stopped
by to get their cars serviced or buy new or used cars. That made my long days
go faster—I often worked from 8:00 a.m. to 8:00 p.m.

Every Christmas Eddie Sr. would throw a big party in Grants, which was
the halfway point between his dealerships in Albuquerque and Gallup. All the
employees of his three dealerships were invited. Great food was provided, and
awards were given to certain employees to recognize their accomplishments
throughout the year. I was fortunate to receive an award every year. At the

Christmas party in 1995 Eddie told me he was glad to have me as part of his team. He always seemed happy to see how many people knew me when they came through his doors at work.

I would be remiss if I didn't give credit to one of my fellow salesmen. Mac Bryant, a retired military officer, really took me under his wing and helped train me. He was the number-one salesman, with his own private office. I would occasionally visit with him, and he would give me several pointers on how to interact and follow up with customers. It really helped me to later become the number-one salesman myself.

In March 1996 Eddie Sr. called me to his office and told me that he was going to have to eliminate my public-relations job. That really shocked me, and I said, "I'm not doing a good job?" He said, "You are doing a great job, but I've got a better job for you. I want you to become a salesman."

I told Eddie that I had never been in sales, and he said, "Yes, you have—all your life. You have been selling yourself for years and doing a great job." I thought about it for a few minutes and agreed to start selling the next day, which was a Saturday.

I couldn't believe how easy it was. I sold about five cars that day! Others were impressed and jokingly attributed it to my "charming personality." I have always been a people person, and even though the dealership was owned by a black man, I was now the first black salesman at a Corley dealership. That day I made almost $2,000. I told myself that I should have been in sales a long time ago! I spent the rest of the year honing my sales skills.

I was successful in selling many cars partly because of the network of friends I had developed over the years. These friends included educators, legislators, members of my church, and members of my Kiwanis Club. The majority of customers came in off the street, but there were other customers I had met before, so I was able to connect with them right away. When people drove onto the lot, my favorite greeting was, "Hi, welcome to Albuquerque Lincoln-Mercury. Do you want to buy a car?" The other salespeople teased me about it, but it worked. And so did I—I worked very hard. Whereas most of the salesmen waited at their desks for customers to come inside, I would go outside and make myself available to answer questions.

During the summer months we had to endure very hot weather. I solved this problem by spending much of the time in the air-conditioned service department and looking outside for potential customers.

I was successful at my job at the Lincoln-Mercury dealership and even thought about opening my own car dealership. I've always been fascinated with cars, and I enjoyed the customers as well. A friend once contacted me with such an opportunity, but he said, "All we're going to sell is trash, junkers." I told him I didn't want to do that. It just didn't sit well with me. I didn't want to sell anything that someone would later regret buying.

Part of that sentiment came as the result of a junker that I was once forced to try to sell. When Hyundai began selling its cars in the United States, their quality was not very good. We received one as a trade-in, and a customer was interested in buying it. What a mistake! During the test drive we got on the freeway, and smoke started coming out from under the hood almost immediately. I told the customer to pull over. Then I had to go and find a pay phone to call the dealership to tell someone to come and get us. We had the car towed back, and the customer said, "I don't want to buy a car from this dealership." I didn't blame him. It was one of the few sales that I lost.

Although I lost a few sales, I was fortunate to be the number-one salesman at the dealership in 1997, 1998, and 1999. It took a lot of hard work and many long days. Everyone at the dealership worked six days a week, but I only worked five, and still I was number one in sales. As a bonus, I was rewarded with several free trips during those years.

One trip that Joy and I took was to Costa Rica. Each year KOB Television sponsored a trip for local businesses that advertised with the station. One year Costa Rica was selected as the location, and about sixty individuals from various businesses around the state traveled there. Eddie Sr. and his wife invited Joy and me, and it was the first time that we had been south of Mexico. We stayed in San Jose, the capital, for a few days, and then embarked on a two-day bus tour of the coast. I was particularly interested in learning about the local economy, which emphasized agriculture (bananas, pineapples, and coffee) and tourism. The trip was filled with great food, shopping, and swimming.

Another vacation I was rewarded with was a trip to Las Vegas, Nevada. Joy and I stayed at the New York–New York Hotel. This trip too was filled with shopping, great eating, and entertainment. One of the shows that we enjoyed was the singer Tom Jones.

I was having a great time working at the Lincoln-Mercury dealership, but the long hours were finally getting to me. I was getting older. Even though I had Wednesdays and Sundays off, I was tired.

I was beginning to think of other work opportunities that didn't require such long work hours. Joy was concerned for my general health and even for my safety, because a few weeks earlier a car salesman at another dealership had been robbed on a test drive. I thought I might be having a similar experience when a twenty-minute test drive turned into an hour, through Tijeras Canyon. I told the customer that we had to get back in twenty minutes, and he just said, "They'll have to wait." To say that I was concerned would be an understatement. Fortunately we returned safely to the dealership, where the man paid cash for the car. I knew then that it was time to look for another job.

In 2000 my good friend Alex Abeyta was running for county treasurer. Alex had been the county manager in the 1980s when I was the county commissioner, so we knew each other very well. One day Alex called me up and told me that if he was elected county treasurer, he wanted me to be one of his assistants. He did win, and he offered me the job as promised. So in early March 2001 I told Eddie Sr. that I was going to leave the car dealership and go back to work for the county. He asked, "Can I do anything to keep you here?" I said, "Unfortunately no," and I thanked him for the opportunity. We parted as friends, and on March 17 I began working in the Bernalillo County Treasurer's office.

CHAPTER 18

Bernalillo County

༡༩

About the time I began working for the Bernalillo County Treasurer's office, the following article in the *Albuquerque Journal* outlined Alex Abeyta's expectations of my job duties:

> Abeyta said Malry will act as his point guard when county officials meet with entities, such as the city of Albuquerque or the school district, for which it collects taxes. Malry will assist with two issues facing the Treasurer's Office: the distribution of taxes to those entities and the reappraisal fee those entities owe the county. Malry and county finance officials will meet with local governments and agencies on April 26, Abeyta said, to answer questions and concerns they have—"I think for too long we've never lobbied these people. We don't know them and they don't know us."
>
> Another project Abeyta is assigning to Malry is the breakdown between title companies, the Clerk's Office, and the Assessor's Office that results in about 15,000 returned tax bills. "I'm going to put Lenton on the road to find out what we can do," Abeyta said.

As the special-projects coordinator for the Bernalillo County Treasurer's office, I worked with the assessor and his staff as well as entities such as the Albuquerque Public Schools, providing them with information on tax matters. I also functioned as a lobbyist for the treasurer at the state legislature.

There were a number of pieces of legislation that I tracked that affected the treasurer's office. I enjoyed this part of the job because I knew many of the legislators from having worked with them in the 1970s. Our lobbying efforts were successful, and I enjoyed working for Alex, a great friend as well as my supervisor.

During this time I got involved with the National Associations of Counties again. I had been on NACO's board of directors during the 1980s when I was a county commissioner, and this time I was appointed to the deferred-compensation board. It primarily oversaw the deferred-compensation program, which provides benefits to county employees in the form of a tax reduction, a savings program, and automatic deductions, all at no cost to the employer.

I enjoyed working with County Commissioner Javier Gonzales, the incoming president of NACO. I had fondly known the Gonzales family since the 1970s when I was a legislator. The family owned a radio station, and I had appeared on several programs to discuss legislative issues. One of the family members was the mayor of Santa Fe from 1968 to 1972. To date, Javier is the only person from New Mexico to have served as president of NACO. He truly deserved it and represented our state well. He is now the mayor of Santa Fe, and we continue to be friends.

The NACO board duties were volunteer work, but I always enjoyed the annual national deferred-compensation board meetings, which I attended for nine years.

In November 2004 Alex ran for reelection but unfortunately lost. Since my job was a political appointment, I served at the will of the current treasurer, and there was no guarantee that I would be retained by his successor. I had made many friends, so I attempted to find another job within county government. The county manager at that time was Thaddeus Lucero, and I had gotten to know him pretty well while I worked in the treasurer's office. I also knew his father, Anthony Lucero, who had served in the state legislature when I was there.

During the summer of 2004 County Commissioner Tom Rutherford had informed me of a job opening in the county manager's office. The county had decided to resurrect the Neighborhood Association Program and needed a coordinator. The job was still open after Alex lost the election, so I applied for it and was selected. It was a full-time position, serving as the liaison for the county manager with the eighty or so neighborhood associations and the local business community. Thaddeus also wanted me to work with our public-information staff to develop methods of disseminating information that promoted county programs and services. The following article in the *Albuquerque Journal* announced my new position:

Former Commissioner Malry has returned to Bernalillo County government and approaches his job of Neighborhood Program Coordinator with the vitality and purpose of a new hire. It is an energy that has served him well. Dr. Malry was Albuquerque's first Negro school principal in 1964, the first black elected to the New Mexico House of Representatives (1968) and first African-American to be elected as Bernalillo County Commissioner (1980).

Some of the neighborhood associations were very small, with maybe only fifteen members, and others were very large, with more than one hundred. The two largest associations were North Albuquerque Acres, located in the Paseo del Norte and Eubank area, and Sandia Heights, located in the north Tramway area. These were the only associations to have full-time staff and strict association laws and covenants.

I began attending various neighborhood-association meetings in the evenings. Some associations, like North Albuquerque Acres, were very active and met once a month. Some, like Sandia Heights, met once a year (but even some of these had monthly subcommittee meetings). I went to at least a dozen meetings a month, and each one usually lasted about two hours. Fortunately for me, there were no meetings scheduled on Friday evenings and only a few scheduled on Saturdays or Sundays. I was therefore able to attend New Mexico Lobos (the UNM athletic teams) sporting events and go to church.

The first meeting I attended was held by the Mountain View Neighborhood Association. I was introduced and spoke on behalf of the county manager and the county commissioners. I said positive things about the county and the services it offered, for ten to fifteen minutes, and then took questions. I repeated that speech hundreds of times in the next six years. We didn't have a county newsletter back then, so I was the sole pitchman for Bernalillo County.

I was also the only black person at most of the meetings. I was usually well received, but there was one negative instance in the East Mountain area. It was an entirely white farming area, and the neighborhood association held its meetings in the community center except for the time I was scheduled to appear. Apparently, when they found out that I'm black they canceled the meeting without telling me. A white man working in his fields simply told me that they weren't meeting that month. I asked why, and he didn't provide an answer. I turned around and went home, and I never went back. I informed my supervisor, who was not very happy about it, and we discussed alternative ways to provide information to the neighborhood. All the neighborhood associations were very good to me except for that group.

In 2005 Governor Bill Richardson appointed me to serve on a search committee to select the first secretary of higher education. Dan Lopez, the president of New Mexico Tech, chaired the committee. We selected Beverlee McClure, who was then the president of Clovis Community College. She served the state well by emphasizing the need to connect institutions of higher education with business and industry needs.

I continued to serve as a deacon at the First Baptist Church. In 2006 our pastor relocated from Albuquerque, so the church elected nine members to a search committee to find his replacement. I was fortunate to be elected vice chairman of the committee. After reviewing more than thirty résumés and watching several videotapes, we believed we had a strong candidate: Pastor Mike Cook of Gilmer, Texas.

Barry Porter, the chairman of the selection committee, and I went to hear Pastor Cook preach in person. We flew to Dallas and then rented a car and drove another 140 miles east to Gilmer. When we arrived in Gilmer, we stopped at a gas station to ask for directions to the Baptist church. They told me how to get to the black Baptist church, so I told them I was talking about the white church. They gave me a funny look, but they did give me the directions. I thought to myself, "Welcome home."

When Barry and I went in the church, the ushers asked us, "Where are you guys from?" We replied that we were just passing through, because we didn't want to let on that we might be hiring their pastor away from them. We sat in the back, and when the service was over we invited Pastor Cook and his wife, Becky, and their daughter, Amber, to have lunch with us in Longview—about twenty-five miles from Gilmer. We had a nice visit and then went back to Albuquerque.

I told Barry right away that I was sold on Pastor Cook. He just seemed like a very intelligent, passionate man, and I was impressed with his family. I believed he would connect well with our congregation.

The following week the church flew Mike and Becky to Albuquerque to be interviewed by the full committee. The meeting, held at my home, consisted of two hours of questions and general discussion. The next morning the church held a breakfast meeting with all the deans of the church, who also asked several questions. I then took Pastor Cook to visit H. B. Horn, one of the elder statesmen and the backbone of the church, and that visit went well. Finally, the pastor met with the senior citizens of the church, who asked several questions.

When I took the Cooks back to the airport, I told them that we really wanted them here in Albuquerque. Although they liked Albuquerque and appreciated the opportunity, they had to consider the fact that their daughter was a senior in high school and didn't want to leave her classmates. Fortunately, Pastor Cook's parents lived in Longview, which meant that Amber could live with them for a year, which she did. Pastor Cook accepted the position and is still with us today, at our new church location on the west side of Albuquerque at 4101 Paseo del Norte NW.

In 2006 I was asked to serve on Governor Richardson's reelection campaign. He wanted me to serve on the finance committee, chaired by Hobbs businessman Johnny Cope, and we met monthly, usually in Albuquerque. After being reelected Governor Richardson asked me to serve on several committees to select judges for the district courts in Albuquerque.

In 2009 Bernadette Miera was hired to oversee the Neighborhood Association Program. I informed the manager that I wanted to work part-time for a few years before I retired. I was able to set my work schedule for Monday, Wednesday, and Thursday because I wanted to have a longer weekend and also because most government holidays fell on Mondays. I worked around twenty-four hours a week at this time. Even on my days off, I still attended the neighborhood association meetings. Bernadette and I divided the list of meetings, and we each took half. Bernadette also started a monthly newsletter.

In 2010 there were some big changes in Bernalillo County. Thaddeus Lucero, the longtime county manager, was relieved of his duties. He was well liked by the county workers, and many of them, including me, were very disappointed when he left.

In July 2011 I gave my six-month notice that I was going to retire. After that some of the neighborhood associations held retirement parties for me at their meetings and gave me small gifts of appreciation. In December the county commission presented me with a proclamation honoring my work.

⁓⁓

During my ten-year tenure with the county, I continued to be involved with education. In 2000 Joy and I were invited by the dean of the UNM College of Education, Viola Florez, to serve on the college's Education Advancement Council. Its mission was to secure more funding from the state legislature to improve the university. Joy and I both had degrees from UNM so we were attractive candidates for the position. In the fall of 2004 we were featured in the UNM quarterly newsletter, where Dr. Florez announced our addition to the council:

> Malry is an excellent person to judge the impact of finances in education.
> In 1964, he was the state's first African-American principal. In 1968,
> he became the first African-American in New Mexico to be elected to
> the New Mexico legislature, serving on the powerful House Finance
> Committee.
>
> His wife, Joy (MA, Elementary Education, 1968), was an elementary
> school teacher at APS for over 30 years. She remembers that establishing
> a kindergarten for all students really had an impact on her classes. In
> 2000, the Malrys joined the College of Education to continue their
> efforts to improve the education of all New Mexicans.

In the same article Dr. Florez provided information on one of the initiatives the council helped develop:

The Family Development Program (FDP) is preparing preschool teachers across the state in the latest reach in child development and learning through the Mind in the Making program. The FDP staff worked hard to get our state selected as one of four pilot sites in the nation and will be training 150 educators from Albuquerque, Laguna Pueblo, and the UNM Children's Campus.

We are a college committed to being an integral part of education in all corners of the state. We are committed to making a difference in how our population lives and the quality of all our people. We are truly working to educate the youth of all ages and all cultural backgrounds in New Mexico.

Joy and I enjoyed serving on the council for more than ten years. We were very impressed and pleased with the leadership of Dr. Florez, and we hope we were able to have a positive effect on our state in some small way.

In 2007 I was pleased to be honored by the Albuquerque community on two occasions. The first was in March, when I received the Living Legend Award from the University of New Mexico's Office of African-American Student Services at the Marsha K. Hardeman Black Cultural Conference in Albuquerque. This award was for my work in the state legislature to create the Sickle-Cell Anemia Council. The second recognition was from my alma mater, Grambling College, now called Grambling State University, which nominated me to its Hall of Fame. Generally, when I think of Halls of Fame, especially at Grambling, athletics come to mind, particularly football. But this Hall of Fame recognized outstanding contributions made by Grambling graduates to society. Apparently some people had recommended me because I was such a strong proponent of education in New Mexico, and in particular for the state legislation I was able to get passed in 1973 to establish all-day kindergartens.

More than twenty letters of support were sent on my behalf, including this one from Governor Richardson on August 28, 2007:

Dr. Malry has served the public as the first black official to the New Mexico legislature House of Representatives, and also the first black elected official to serve as a Bernalillo County Commissioner. While serving in the state legislature, from 1968–1978, he passed the Sickle Cell bill to help provide for education and screenings throughout the black communities of New Mexico. Additionally, Dr. Malry helped pass the Statewide Kindergarten Bill, when in 1973, the States of New Mexico, Mississippi, and Alabama were the only states in the country that had not yet provided for this education.

Most recently, I appointed Dr. Malry to serve on several of my advisory committees, including Higher Education Search and Campaign Finance. Please give Dr. Malry every allowable consideration under your rules and guidelines for induction to the Grambling State University Hall of Fame.

The following letter was from UNM President Bud Davis, dated August 26, 2007:

As a friend and educational colleague of Dr. Malry (who was a part-time adjunct professor of political science at UNM), I was intrigued and impressed by the fact he was elected to both state and county political office in predominantly white neighborhoods, which is worthy testament to the respect and confidence placed in him regardless of the cultural background of his constituencies.

And this letter came from my church pastor, Michael Cook, dated August 23, 2007:

I have had the opportunity to serve as Dr. Malry's pastor for the past two years. I can testify to his amazing heart. As Senior Pastor, [I] find very few people with such a willingness and enthusiastic approach in helping others. When students could not afford to attend summer camp, Dr. Malry reached into his own pocket to provide the financial resources to make available a great camp experience for many of our students. When there has been a benevolent need, Dr. Malry [has been] the first to step forward to help someone.

That year twelve people were admitted to Grambling's Hall of Fame, including me. I was proud to have Pastor Cook join me at Grambling for the induction ceremony on October 1. Some of the other honorees at that ceremony had also done good work in their respective communities, such as Rayford Richard, a physician from Jackson, Mississippi; Otto Meyers, an attorney from Houston; Everson Walls, an ex-football player with the Dallas Cowboys; Richard Gallot, a state representative from Grambling and Ruston; and Yvonne McLintosh, a professor at Florida A&M University.

In the spring of 2008 Joy and I passed a significant milestone: we celebrated our fiftieth wedding anniversary. We wanted to go on a cruise, but we didn't know where. We had already been to the Bahamas twice and to Alaska and Canada, so I said, "Let's go to southern Europe." We set out for Italy, Croatia, and Greece on a twelve-day Mediterranean Romance Cruise with the Holland America Cruise Line. We left Albuquerque on July 18, 2008, and had a fantastic time, enjoying great food, shopping, and sight-seeing.

When we got home, however, I began experiencing shortness of breath, and I got tired easily. I went to my doctor, and he immediately sent me to see a heart specialist who conducted a stress test that determined something was terribly wrong. The next morning I was in surgery. One of my arteries was blocked, and a stent had to be inserted to restore proper blood flow. As they were putting me under anesthesia, the surgeon, Kathleen Allen, told me to relax and joked that I had nothing to worry about because she was a big supporter of Barack Obama (who was then running for his first term as president). I found out that she already knew me. She had gone to Sandia High School in Albuquerque when I was in the state legislature, had studied in New York, and had then come back to Albuquerque to practice. The operation and recovery went well—I had a great group of individuals at Presbyterian Hospital caring for me.

CHAPTER 19

Life after Retirement

~*~

I n January 2012 I had just begun my retirement and was having a difficult time adjusting to it. I had nothing to do. Going through the same morning routine of retrieving the newspaper and observing my neighbors going off to work was strange. I said to myself, "What am I doing at home? I feel well, but I'm not being productive."

I like to stay active, always moving from one place to another. Joy tried to help by putting me to work with a lot of projects around the house. But that was not necessarily my interest. To maintain my health, I would visit the health spa every day except Sunday to exercise. I have been a member of the Sports and Wellness gym in Albuquerque for many years, so I was used to going there every day during my lunch hour. When I was working full-time, I would quickly work out during my lunch hour, pick up something to eat, and take it back to my office. I was always in a big rush because I had to do everything in an hour. But once I retired there was no rush. I could stay at the gym for several hours.

A daily workout at the gym is not only for physical exercise but also for socializing with friends. One of those is attorney and former legislator Raymond Sanchez. We served together in the legislature in the 1970s, so we often discuss politics and the challenges his brother, Senator Michael Sanchez, now faces as a leader of the state senate. I also keep track of current news events by watching television while running on the treadmill.

I am still active in the First Baptist Church. In the 1970s I led the Royal

Ambassadors youth program and taught high school seniors, and currently I am the head usher and the vice chairman of the deacons (formally the head deacon). Joy and I attend church services on Sunday and Wednesday. We also enjoy traveling with other senior members of the church. As a group, we have visited Santa Fe and Vancouver, Canada, which was a fun vacation.

My interest in real estate has also provided me with a productive retirement activity. I started buying property in Rio Rancho in the 1980s and had accumulated quite a few lots. I got into real estate after Joy and I built a new home in Albuquerque and decided to rent out our first one. Renting was a pain, so three years later I sold the house. The money I made on the deal I invested in property in Rio Rancho. It proved to be a good investment— that property allowed me to purchase additional land. By 1998 I had more than sixty lots. Later a local developer named Chuck Hagen purchased all but twenty of my lots. I sold more property over the years, but I still own several acres.

My brother in Shreveport was a realtor, and my brother in California owned apartments and laundromats. Through the experiences I had with buying and selling my own property, I decided to attend real-estate school and even obtained my license. I went to auction sales on foreclosed land, but I didn't buy and sell for others. I simply enjoyed working in real estate. All this kept me busy.

I think it helped me as a realtor that I had been the county commissioner in the 1980s. Many people knew me, so when I told them that I wanted to buy their property to build a house on it, they figured that would be okay. That's a far cry from what I had experienced in the 1960s and 1970s, when almost no one wanted Joy and me to live in their neighborhoods.

I continue to be politically active. I'm a member of the New Mexico Democratic State Central Committee. I was also appointed by Bernalillo County Commissioner Maggie Hart Stebbins to serve on the county's seven-member Planning and Zoning Committee. We meet to consider zoning requests and make recommendations to the county commission. The long public comments remind me of my time serving as county commissioner.

For example, we recently considered a case regarding a local Boy Scout troop that wanted to buy a small piece of land for a campsite in the East Mountain area. The residents were against it; they complained that the campsite would produce too much noise and traffic and even be a fire hazard. I said to myself, "Really? Where else would you put Boy Scouts in training?" It was ridiculous. This work is voluntary, but I do enjoy serving my community.

I continue to be an active member of the Kiwanis Club, which I have belonged to for more than thirty-five years. Now that I am not working, I have more opportunity to attend meetings and events. One of my favorite fund-raising events is the annual pancake breakfast. Typically well attended, the event was held at La Cueva High School this year. Although I've helped cook the pancakes, I usually just serve coffee and juice. One of my favorite joke lines is "Coffee, tea, or me?" a reference to a 1973 movie about a stewardess. I have a great time talking with people and socializing while benefiting a great cause.

Joy and I have been big New Mexico Lobos boosters for years. I started attending games in the 1970s as a state representative, as a way to network and campaign, but I've always loved sports. Joy and I have held season tickets for both football and basketball games for more than forty years. We first began attending Lobos basketball games when the team played in Johnson Gymnasium and Bob King was the head coach. Coach King had a star player named Ira Harge, who after college played professionally for several years. During his senior year at UNM, Harge was assigned to student-teach at Lincoln Junior High School, where I was a teacher. We became friends then and continue to be to this day.

When Norm Ellenberger was the coach, the Lobo Club, of which I was a member, asked me for assistance in recruiting a star basketball player from Virginia. I was flattered and agreed to travel with some club representatives to Virginia. We saw this phenomenal player, Moses Malone, in an informal, spontaneous game, and he played like a man among boys. There were several major university representatives in attendance. We connected very well with Malone's mother, a nurse's aid, but she was concerned with the distance from Virginia to New Mexico, which meant that she would not be able to see her son very often.

Malone's other college choice was in Maryland, and his third option was to turn pro, which is what he did. After graduating from high school he opted to play for the Utah Stars of the American Basketball Association, a rival league of the National Basketball Association (NBA). Malone played professionally for twenty-one years, including nineteen in the NBA. He was a three-time NBA Most Valued Player (MVP) and was named one of the NBA's fifty greatest players. He earned an NBA championship ring and finals MVP trophy in 1983 with the Philadelphia 76ers. I've often wondered what the Lobos would look like today if we had signed him.

Joy and I also attended Lobos football games when they were played on the UNM campus before University Stadium was built. Today we are still avid fans, as is Lenny, who keeps us informed on the latest inside news about the Lobos.

On October 4, 2012, I was honored to receive the UNM Black Alumni Chapter's Trailblazer Award, recognizing me for being New Mexico's first black state representative. Two other individuals were also honored: James Lewis, the first black state treasurer, in 1986; and Angela Juzang Jewell, New Mexico's first black female district judge, elected in 1996 and reelected in 2006, 2008, and 2010.

The event was a small, intimate gathering of about forty people. I was proud to have Lenny introduce me, and here is part of what he said:

> This award goes to an individual who accomplished many firsts, a pioneer, a leader within the black community here in New Mexico. My father has exemplified these "firsts" in the areas of education, public service, and elective office. Several of these are noted in his biography listed in your program.

I could tell he was touched, since he began tearing up while speaking. After Lenny's introduction, I said a few words, and we had our pictures taken. This is the biography that appeared in the program:

> Dr. Lenton Malry enjoyed a very successful and fulfilling career in public service, academia, and the private sector. His focus has always been to protect the rights and improve the quality of life for the people of New Mexico. Dr. Malry served as New Mexico's first African-American State Representative from 1968–78 and Bernalillo County's first African-American Commissioner—serving as commission chairman in 1983–1984 and 1987–88. He had an enormous influence in changing

New Mexico from a state where, in 1962, covenants were still in place restricting African-Americans from purchasing a home, to a state where diversity is respected and celebrated. As an educator, Malry served our community's children for more than 25 years by working as a teacher as well as a human resources director, a cultural awareness director, a student advisor, and most notably Albuquerque's first African-American principal, retiring from APS in 1987. As a business owner, Malry served as president of Malry and Associates, a consulting firm. Dr. Malry received his bachelor's degree from Grambling State University, his Master's in Education from Texas College, and a Ph.D. in Educational Administration from the University of New Mexico in 1968.

On November 3, 2012, I was also honored by the Sickle-Cell Anemia Council of New Mexico. I was provided with a plaque that says the following:

The Sickle Cell Council of New Mexico presents this award to Lenton Malry in grateful appreciation for his vision, commitment, and support for the establishment of the Sickle Cell Council of New Mexico 40 years ago. Thank you, Board of Directors/Staff.

I was honored by the Kiwanis Club in August 2013 for having been a member for more than 35 years. The other honorees included then mayoral candidate Pete Dinelli, State Treasurer James Lewis, and Financial Advisor Paulette Read (the first female honoree, which was long overdue).

A couple of weeks later I had the opportunity to go back home to Shreveport, Louisiana. My cousin Janie Mae and my niece picked me up at the airport. After Joy and I checked into the hotel, we went to see my first-grade teacher, Mrs. Curliff, who lives with her daughter. She was small and a little hunched over, but she didn't use a cane. Mrs. Curliff attends the same church as Janie Mae, and on October 30, 2012, she turned 102 years old! She told me that she had worn out three husbands! I really enjoyed visiting with her. We took pictures and talked about when she was my teacher in the first grade. She remembered that I was very social and didn't want to stay in my seat. She also fondly recalled the whipping she gave me—when I went home and told my dad, and he gave me another whipping.

We left around 3:00 p.m. and drove to John Gin Road. Our first stop there was at the home of Irma Bennett. Her brother, Booker T., had come up from Lake Charles, Louisiana, to see me. Then we all drove to Spring Ridge, about five minutes away. We had lots of fun talking about the time we were in school together. We went to the area where our school used to be, but it's not there anymore. However, the church and the black cemetery are still there, so we took more pictures. I am sure I have some relatives buried there.

When I grew up there, all that land was just farms and dirt roads. Now it is a suburb of Shreveport, a nice subdivision with paved streets and very nice homes. Blacks and whites now live next door to each other without any problems. It was encouraging to see.

CHAPTER 20

Looking Back, Looking Forward

ʟ⁓

L ooking back, I can attribute the good
fortune I've experienced to many
things, not the least of which is the Lord. As improbable as my journey may
seem, all things are possible with Him.

One key to my success was a firm belief in and commitment to education.
In our poor family, this principle was instilled by my mother, who knew that
education was a must for a black person to be economically viable, and she
demonstrated her commitment to this by doing whatever it took to make it
a reality for me. This belief in the value of education was further reinforced
for me by the Bennett family, who provided transportation to grade school
for me and assisted in my transition to college the first year. In addition, Jack
Sheehan provided strong words of encouragement and positive reinforcement
while I was in the air force, and my wife continually supported me in my
pursuit of advanced, graduate-level education.

My belief in the benefits of education was supplemented with a keen sense
of adventure, instilled by my brothers by their enlistment in the military. In
addition, I had a strong desire to leave the segregated South, especially after
living in England and experiencing racial integration there. Finally, my drive
and dedication to hard work was given to me by my father. Every day he
demonstrated a commitment to provide for his family by performing hard
manual labor, which was the way of life, without complaining.

Given this experience, I chose to pursue education as a profession. I had
seen the benefits of education firsthand, and I wanted to improve the lives

of others, especially children. Elective office was a vehicle for achieving this strategy on a large scale. Although I lost my first and last elections, I was successful in several others, becoming the first black official to serve in all the races I won. But it wasn't necessarily all about being the first black person elected; it was about being effective. Regardless of what obstacles may exist, one can overcome them with a clear and sound message. The other firsts that I achieved were also important, not necessarily for me but for other blacks and minorities, especially children, to realize that through education one can accomplish much.

"Do nothing out of selfish ambition or vain conceit. Rather, in humility value others above yourselves," says Philippians 2:3.

As I look forward, our country faces many challenges and continues to wrestle with economic disparity among ethnic groups and, in general, with race relations. Although the country has made great strides in race relations—evident in the integration of neighborhoods, churches, and the workplace and in the election of a black president—there are many examples of hatred based on race. There is a platform given to this vocal minority in the form of conservative television, talk radio, and social media.

But as I've gotten older, I've come to the opinion that even though race relations matter, economic segregation is the major issue we must address, especially as it relates to education. Education is the great equalizer. Our country has always prided itself on being the land of opportunity, where hard work and sacrifice result in a better life. Economic growth has made that opportunity a reality for many in this country, including those like me who began poor.

Of concern are the increasing gaps in academic achievement and educational attainments, especially among low-income children and children of color in relation to higher-income and white children. Math and reading levels, as well as graduation rates, are markedly lower in the first two groups than in the latter two, and the differences have gotten larger over several decades.

This is an economic issue, not only at the individual level but also for society as a whole. There are enough resources available, but we are not efficient in our use of them. People are spending significant amounts of money for an education, with mixed results. Meanwhile, few societal resources are spent on supportive and social services; instead, crime and incarceration are the focus.

True educational reform is needed. We need to create a system that is less dependent on parental support and where barriers to access are minimized and even eliminated. This system would value quality teaching in the form of increased compensation and would provide technology and quality resources. We need a system in which business and industry are involved, since they are the ultimate arbiter in what skills are and will be needed to compete globally. If this means longer school days and year-round schooling, then I'm all for it. There are several examples around the world of highly successful educational systems, and those examples could be utilized here, if we had the collective will to implement change. This is a critical issue that must be solved. Our future is at stake. So let's stop talking about this, and let's roll this train!